EXPLORING
THE
OLD TESTAMENT

A Guidebook for the Study of the Bible

By RACHEL HENDERLITE

John Knox Press

ATLANTA

FIFTEENTH PRINTING 1983

COPYRIGHT 1945 • JOHN KNOX PRESS • ATLANTA

PRINTED IN U.S.A.

INTERNATIONAL STANDARD BOOK NUMBER: 0-8042-0120-X

FOREWORD TO THE STUDENT

THESE sheets are planned as guides to help you in your study of the Old Testament—to help you to explore the lives of men and women of the past as they have found God and have learned to build their lives around their knowledge of Him. The sheets will help you to get the facts about these people, but they will also ask questions to make you think about their religious problems, and yours; because it is believed that you will not be satisfied with a religious outlook which is based on mere information *about* the Bible. The facts about the Bible and about the people in it are necessary as a part of your religious heritage, but you must think these facts through and relate them to your own problems if you are to get the greatest value from your Bible study. Many of the questions that are raised you may not be able to answer completely before coming to class; but if you think them through carefully, you will be able to participate in the classroom discussion and you will probably be able to help your fellow students on some problems, while they will be able to help you on others. Your teacher will attempt to guide all of you into a deeper understanding of many of these religious problems which have been bothering you for a long time.

Let these guide sheets lead you into the exciting experience of discovering God for yourself; for you can discover Him best as He deals with people and tries to lead them into a knowledge of Himself and His world, and His great purpose for mankind. Let them help you to see what God has meant to other people as they have tried to live in the midst of a world not at all unlike our own world. Let them show you how God revealed more and more about Himself to men until finally they were prepared for His supreme revelation of Himself in Jesus Christ. And as you discover these great unfolding truths about God, many of you can be led into a knowledge and experience of Him that will be as great and satisfying for you as it has proved to be for these men and women you will read about in the Old Testament.

Since you will not want to limit yourself to the guide sheets, but will want to make a notebook containing other types of work, holes have been punched so that if you remove these sheets you can insert them in your Bible notebook. Then you can be proud of a record of your own learning experience. Try not to let yourself be cramped by the mechanical arrangement of these pages. You will want to turn back to this book many times for your own enjoyment, or for rethinking some of these problems. Remember! Your notebook is what you make of it; it reflects the sort of person you are and the sort of person you are becoming.

FOREWORD TO THE TEACHER

THESE guide sheets are studies in the Old Testament planned with the purpose of raising definite religious problems which high school students are facing. The problems are not artificially imposed upon the material but arise from the Old Testament situations, and are to be studied by the class in the Old Testament setting. Each guide sheet raises its own problem and deals with its own block of material, but is at the same time closely related to the unit of study in which it is found. Thus there is a twofold purpose here: a mastery of the facts of the Bible and an understanding of these facts as they relate to each other and as they may prove to be a guide to living in the present day. The teacher will be most helpful if he will seek to present the historical data to the student in such a way as to make clear its implications for personal and social living.

More material is given here than can be covered in the time allotted to Old Testament study in many schools. But because of the form of the book it will be easy to omit whole units and select other units for more concentrated study than is indicated on the guide sheets. For example, Unit III on Leviticus and Unit V on Deuteronomy are marked "Optional," as units which may be omitted without disturbing the historical continuity of the story of Israel. It will be obvious at once that the "poetic books" have been completely omitted from this material (except for a brief glance at some of the Psalms and one guide sheet on Proverbs), and that the prophets are treated in a very summary fashion. It was felt necessary to make some adjustment of this kind because of the limitation of time in most high schools, and it was felt that the greatest value might come from a study of the historical books for a background of Hebrew history, leaving the prophets and the great poetic books for more advanced study at a later time. Teachers preferring to give more attention to these sections of the Old Testament in this introductory study should feel free to amplify the relevant sections of the guidebook.

Suggestions for the Use of the Guide Sheets

The guide sheets are designed as assignment sheets for the use of the pupil. They are planned to lead him directly into a firsthand study of the text of the Bible. They may be used to direct his individual study outside of class, in which case the teacher will base the class discussion on the guide sheet assigned. Or they may be used in the classroom as the basis of directed study, either by the class as a whole or by the students working individually. The work book should be thought of as a laboratory manual for stimulating and directing the student's work. It should be a means of study and not an end in itself. Therefore the inaccuracy of an answer is significant only in so far as it indicates lack of careful thought on the part of the student; and the student's answers to questions in the guidebook should be considered merely as preliminary to group discussion. Few teachers will find them a satisfactory basis for grading.

It will be necessary for the teacher to supplement this material and work out his own method of conducting the class session. Several procedures have proved valuable in the classroom in connection with this material, and these are appended here as suggestions for inexperienced teachers.

1. Checking the factual questions on the guide sheets either individually or by the class as a group so that the students may have accurate information on which to base the further work of the class.

2. Leading the class in discussion of all the questions which require reflection and represent student opinions.

3. Telling the story of the incident upon which the questions are based. If this is done, care should be taken to avoid repetition of the preparation the students have already made. The story may be enriched with imaginative and vivid details and elements of the story stressed which have bearing on the problem posed at the beginning of the guide sheet.

4. Using informal dramatization in class with those lessons which lend themselves to it: the story of Joseph, the story of the Gibeonites and Joshua, and the book of Ruth, to mention only a few.

5. Bringing music, poetry, and art into the classroom to enrich the material under consideration. Some of the things that can be used with the average group are such Negro spirituals as "Go Down, Moses," and "Joshua Fit the Battle of Jericho"; Byron's "The Assyrian Came Down Like a Wolf on the Fold"; Browning's "Saul"; Michelangelo's "Moses," etc.

6. Showing moving pictures or film slides from time to time to draw together a whole unit of study, or to review a long period of Old Testament history.

7. Testing the student from time to time to assure careful preparation. Tests may be purely factual in nature, and many teachers find it valuable to give five- or ten-minute check-up tests of this kind each day. However, longer and more comprehensive tests may be used as learning experiences at the end of units of study, to help the student summarize whole movements of history, and to guide his understanding and appreciation of the religious values involved.

8. Urging the students to do creative work either inside or outside of class. Many of them will surprise you with the poems, plays, sketches, illustrated notebooks, etc., which they will produce with some enthusiastic encouragement from the teacher. Suggestions for individual projects will be found at the end of the guidebook.

It is strongly urged that each class hour be utilized to lead the student into one new insight. If the teacher can be very clear in his own mind as to what he wants to accomplish with each hour, he can then select from the above methods of teaching and from others the one or two which will be most effective with his class. Help the student to enjoy the class period. Let him feel free to bring up for discussion other problems which concern him. Make each class session one which shows the relevance of religion to the lives of Old Testament persons and of persons who are living today.

Suggested Books for Supplementary Study

Although there is no teacher's guide especially prepared for assistance in teaching this course, there are a number of books which will prove helpful, if not indispensable, to the teacher. The following is a suggestive list:

Anderson, Bernhard W., *Understanding the Old Testament.*

Anderson, Bernhard W., *Rediscovering the Bible.*

Bailey, Albert Edward, and Kent, Charles Foster, *History of the Hebrew Commonwealth.*

Bright, John, *The Kingdom of God.*

Browne, Lewis, *The Graphic Bible.*

Davis, John D., *The Westminster Dictionary of the Bible* (revised and rewritten by Henry Snyder Gehman).

Dummelow, J. R. (Ed.), *A Commentary on the Holy Bible.*

Freedman, David Noel, and Smart, James D., *God Has Spoken.*

James, Fleming, *Personalities of the Old Testament.*

Kelly, Balmer H. (Ed.), *The Layman's Bible Commentary*

Mould, Elmer W. K., *Essentials of Bible History.*

Westminster Historical Atlas to the Bible. Edited by George Ernest Wright and Floyd Vivian Filson.

The compiler of this book will welcome criticisms and suggestions from any teachers or students who may use the material. This particular form of guide sheet is offered experimentally to help teachers discover another way of presenting the Old Testament dynamically to high school students.

The guidebook could not have been prepared without the help of a number of persons. Dr. Joseph M. Gettys has given such valuable help as to make co-authorship a not untrue statement of his relationship to it. Many of the suggestions of present-day applications of the Old Testament material are his.

A number of teachers of high school Bible courses have used this material in mimeographed form, and have given me the benefit of their classroom experience. Among these are Miss Bowers MacKorell of Charlotte, North Carolina, and my sister, Mrs. Frank S. Jones, of Asheboro, North Carolina, both of whom have helped materially by unfailing criticism, for which I am grateful. I should like to express appreciation also to Dean Luther A. Weigle and Dr. Paul H. Vieth, of Yale Divinity School, who read parts of the manuscript and made helpful suggestions at various points.

A special word of thanks is due to former classes of mine in Harding High School and Charlotte Technological High School, Charlotte, North Carolina, and to my classes in Prospect Hill School in New Haven, Connecticut. In all three cases has the criticism of students been forthcoming—and very valuable indeed.

Very especial appreciation is expressed to Miss Athalie Lindler for her drawing of the maps in the guidebook and to Miss Mary Virginia Robinson for her assistance in preparing the material for printing. Finally, my thanks are due to Mr. Robert Clark for his assistance in typing the manuscript.

RACHEL HENDERLITE

TABLE OF CONTENTS

The Beginning of Things

HOW THE WORLD CAME TO BE

How did we get here? How much did the Hebrews know about the beginning of the world? What kind of God did they believe in?

Read Genesis 1 three or four times. Read it once aloud.

1. List the things that were created in the order of creation.
   (1) .... (3) .... (5) ....
   (2) .... (4) .... (6) ....

2. Do you find evidence that the creation was orderly, that there was progress of any kind?
   ....

3. List several phrases in the chapter that you find repeated many times.
   (1) .... (3) ....
   (2) .... (4) ....

4. Is there any indication of the date of the creation of the world?
   ....

5. Count the number of times you find the word GOD or LORD..
   How do you account for the frequent occurrence of the word?..
   ....

6. From your study of the chapter, what things do you discover that the Hebrews knew positively about the beginning of the world?..
   ....

7. What does the chapter not tell you that you would like to know?..
   ....

8. Think over the chapter carefully to see whether you can decide what was the main thing the author was trying to get across..
   ....

9. What adjectives best describe God as you find Him in this chapter?
   (1) .... (3) .... (5) ....
   (2) .... (4) .... (6) ....

10. Make a note of any questions that you would like to have the class discuss. Has this chapter raised any questions in your mind?
   ....
   ....

WHAT IS MAN LIKE?

What is man like? What is he capable of becoming? Why does he so often fail? Under what conditions can he be used by God?

1. List everything in chapters 1—4 which suggests that man was the greatest thing created, or the end of creation.

   (1) .... (3) .... (5) ....

   (2) .... (4) .... (6) ....

   What do you think it means to be created "in the image of God"?

2. In what way were Adam and Eve like us? ....

   ....

3. What were the results of their disobedience? List as many as you can discover..................

   ....

   ....

4. Try to figure out why Abel's offering was better than Cain's. Read Genesis 4:6, 7 and

   Hebrews 11:4. Express in your own words...

   ....

5. What caused Cain to murder Abel?..

6. Of what other sins was Cain guilty? (4:5)...........................(4:9)...........................

7. What would you say *sin* is?...

8. Read Genesis 4:25, 26 for information about the third son of Adam and Eve. What was

   the attitude of this man and his family toward God? ....

   ....

   ....

9. Which son of Adam and Eve will be most useful to future generations of man?..................

   Why? ....

10. If we had only Genesis 1—4, what would we know about how to live? About how not to

    live? ....

    ....

    ....

WHAT GOD EXPECTS OF MAN

How does God feel about wrongdoing?

Read Genesis 6—9 and 11:1-9.

1. List phrases from chapter 6 that show the wickedness of the people.

    (1) ....
    (2) ....
    (3) ....
    (4) ....
    (5) ....
    (6) ....

2. In what ways was Noah different from the other people of his time?

   ....

   ....

3. Was it difficult for Noah to trust in God under these circumstances? .... Try to discover the things that show this trust. ....

4. What sort of world did God want Noah to build after the floods had disappeared? ....
   .... List several important commands He gave Noah about this new world.

   ....

   ....

5. What is a "covenant"? (Look up in a dictionary) ....

   ....

6. What would this covenant sign of the rainbow always mean to Noah and his children?

   ....

7. What were some of the things that Noah found out about God from his own experience?

   ....

   ....

8. When Noah failed to live up to the best he knew, which of his sons proved most worthy of the trust that God had put in this family? ....

9. Try to discover what was wrong with building the tower of Babel.

   ....

   ....

A BACKWARD AND A FORWARD VIEW

What is the importance of these early stories of the Hebrews for us today?

1. List five examples of wrongdoing in chapters 1—11.

    (1)..

    (2)..

    (3)..

    (4)..

    (5)..

2. List the occasions when men gave themselves to God to do right.

    (1)..

    (2)..

    (3)..

3. Does your definition of sin still satisfy you?..

    If not, try to write a new one on the basis of thcsc eleven chapters. ....

    ....

    ....

4. Locate the following events by chapters. What does each show about God?

	Chapter	*Teaching about God*
Creation	....	....
Punishment of Adam and Eve	....	....
Rejecting Cain's offering	....	....
God's care of Noah	....	....
The rainbow	....	....

5. List the men with whom God has been able to work successfully in these chapters.................

    ....

6. Glance through chapter 10. Is it interesting to you?................. Would that kind of material

    be more interesting if you found it in your family Bible?................. Why?.........................

    ....

7. Can you begin to see in what direction the book of Genesis is going? What man in chapter

    12 do these first 11 chapters seem to be leading up to?.. **You**

    may rightly suspect that this man is going to be important in God's plans for the future

    world.

ABRAHAM, THE FOUNDER OF A NATION

What qualities would you expect to find in a man whom God would choose as a partner in rebuilding the world? Has Abraham these qualities? Try to discover through the rest of Genesis how God works with people and through people.

1. Where was Abraham born?... Look up on a map. This was a great city of culture.

2. What did Abraham's people worship? (Joshua 24:2) ....

3. Did he move away for political, economic, or religious reasons? (Acts 7:1-4)....................
    ....

4. What must have been his feeling toward the gods of his people?.......................................
    ....

5. Go back to Genesis 11:27-32 for the following information about Abraham:

    His father .... His brothers..............................

    His wife.............................. His nephew ....

    The town to which his father moved..............................

6. What three things did God promise Abraham in 12:2, 3?

    ...., ..., ...

7. List the places where Abraham went in chapters 12—14 and the event that occurred in each place.

    Place   *Event*

    12:6 ....

    12:8 ....

    12:10 ....

    13:3, 4 ....

    13:18 ....

    Put an x beside the events in which Abraham failed God.

8. Do you respect his treatment of his nephew Lot?................ Why?.......................
    ....

9. What qualities of leadership does Abraham show in chapter 14?.......................
    ....

Do you think Abraham will live up to what God expects of him? Can God use an imperfect man? Under what conditions?

THE LAND THAT WAS PROMISED

If your family were to move from your present home, what would determine where they would decide to live?

1. What are some of the questions Abraham would have asked about this land to which he was called? Make a list of at least 10. See whether you can find in an atlas or geography book the information he would have wanted. Let your imagination work!

   (1) Its size: ....
   (2) ....
   (3) ....
   (4) ....
   (5) ....
   (6) ....
   (7) ....
   (8) ....
   (9) ....
   (10) ....
   (11) ....

2. This piece of land has been called "The Bridge of the World." What two great centers of civilization does it connect? ....
   ....

3. How does this fact make it a good piece of land for a "Promised Land"? ....
   ....

4. On Map I label each of the continents and oceans. Draw a circle around the "Promised Land." Locate yourself by putting a cross (x) on the map to show where you live.

5. On Map II locate and label each of the following natural landmarks around the Promised Land:

(1) The Mediterranean Sea	(4) The Euphrates River
(2) The Nile River	(5) The Jordan River
(3) The Tigris River	(6) The Arabian Desert

   Locate the following countries and cities:

(1) Egypt	(3) Canaan
(2) Ur of the Chaldees	(4) Haran

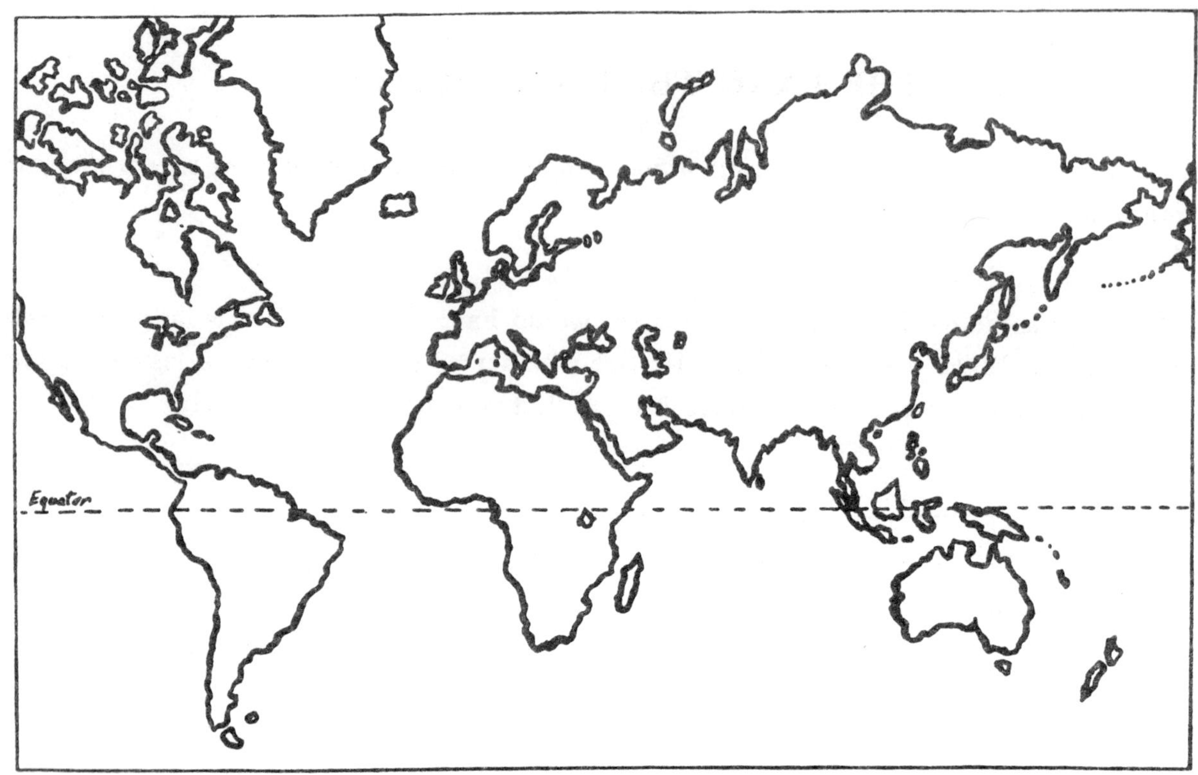

MAP I   *The Promised Land and the World of Today*

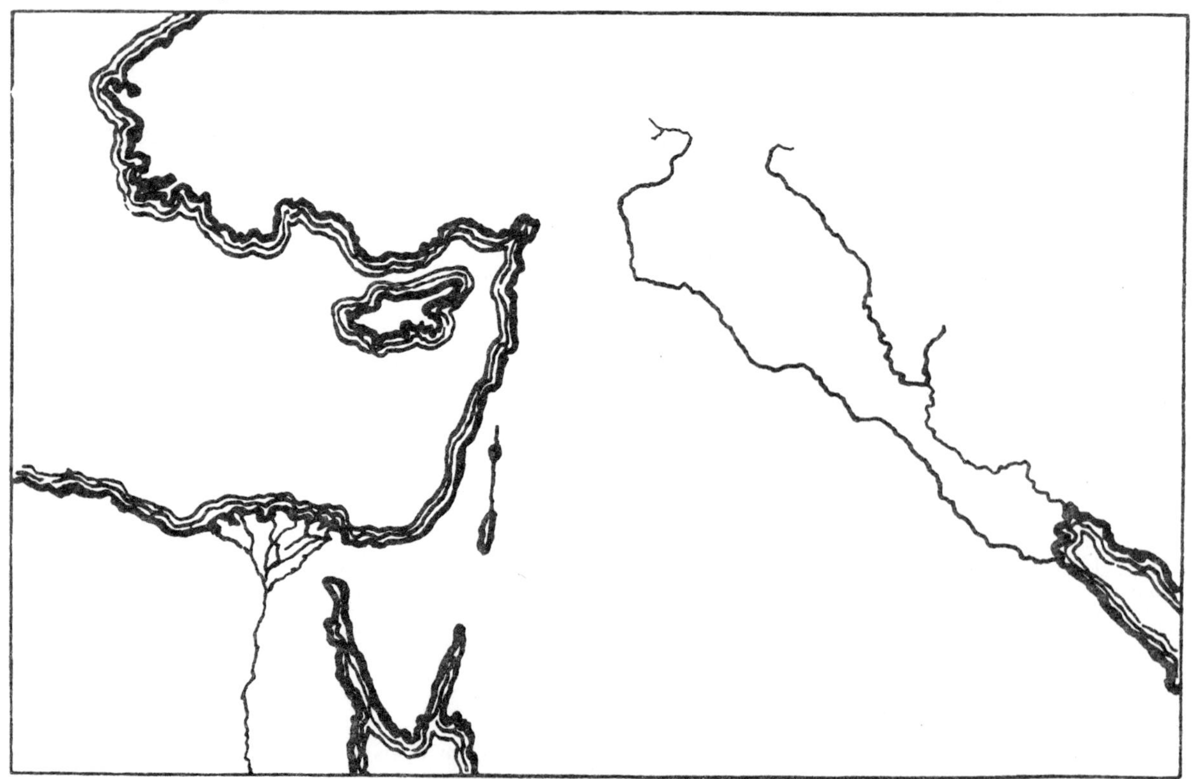

MAP II   *The World of Abraham*

GOD'S COVENANT WITH ABRAHAM

How can a man be sure that God exists and is talking with him?

Read Genesis 15—17.

1. In spite of his riches, what was the one thing that Abraham wanted?

2. Who would be heir of his riches if he had no son? (15:2, 3)

3. Note the figure of speech by which God assured Abraham that he would have children of his own. (15:5)

4. Genesis 15:12-21 is a vision in which God showed Himself to Abraham. A customary way of signing a covenant or contract in the days of Abraham was for the two parties to the contract to pass between the halves of animals that had been divided in two. What reason can you think of for God's revealing Himself as a torch passing between the halves of these animals?

5. How did Abraham try, in chapter 16, to help God fulfill His promise?

   How long had he waited for God to fulfill it? (16:3)

6. Read chapter 17 carefully several times. This is often called "The Covenant Chapter." How many times does the word "covenant" appear in the chapter?

7. How much time had passed since God called Abraham? You can tell by comparing Abraham's age at certain points.

   12:4 .... 16:16 .... 17:1 ....

   Can you think of any reason for God's making Abraham wait all these years for the son he so much wanted?

8. What are the two parts of the Covenant?

   As for me, I WILL (17:4-8)

   As for thee, THOU SHALT (17:9-11)

9. What is the meaning of "Abraham"?

   What is the meaning of "Sarah"?

   Why did God change their names?

THE COVENANT SON

How much does it cost to be partners with God?

Read Genesis 21 and 22.

1. How long had Abraham waited for the birth of Isaac? (21:5) ....

2. What does the name "Isaac" mean? (17:19) ....
   What was the point of giving the name to this boy? ....
   ....

3. What difference did his birth make to Ishmael, Hagar's son? ....
   ....

4. How do you account for the difference in the treatment of the two boys? What was the importance of Isaac in the new world which this family was to help build? ....
   ....

5. Read chapter 22 carefully. What could have been the purpose of the sacrifice of this covenant son upon whom the future depended? ....
   Don't be satisfied with a superficial answer. Think into all the possible meanings—to God, to Abraham.

6. How do you account for Abraham's being willing to do this thing? What had his own experience taught him about God? ....
   ....

7. Try to discover as many things as possible about God from this experience.
   What does He *require* of the men He uses? ....
   What does He *make* of the men He uses? ....

8. What changes have taken place in Abraham in these years of his partnership with God?
   In what ways is he *better off*? ....
   ....
   In what ways is he *better*? ....
   ....

A ROMANCE OF SHEPHERD DAYS

How do people select a wife nowadays? How like or unlike the way Isaac got his?

Read Genesis 24—26.

1. Make a list of the differences between Isaac's marriage and one in America today.
   (1) Selecting a wife
   (2) The gifts of the suitor
   (3) The proposal
   (4) The acceptance
   (5) The wedding trip

2. If you were to dramatize this romance, what characters would you choose?.......................
   ....

   What events would you actually present on the stage and which would you tell about in conversation?

ON STAGE	IN CONVERSATION
....	....
....	....
....	....

3. What relation was Rebekah to Isaac?........................ Why was it so important for Isaac **to** get the right wife?...
   ....

4. List everything that shows that God was guiding Isaac in this choice of a wife................
   ....

5. What did God promise Isaac? (Chapter 26).. ....

6. List everything in chapter 26 that shows you the character of Isaac.
   ....
   ....

7. What characteristics of Isaac would make him a desirable husband?................................
   ....
   ....

8. Why do you think Rebekah would make a good wife?...
   ....

JACOB, THE CHEATER WHO GOT CHEATED

Do you know people who live life for what they can get out of it? Have you ever been tempted to cheat for something you wanted? What sort of things? Can cheating help you to develop personality traits that are worth while?

Chapter 25:19-34

1. Read chapter 25:19-34 quickly to get the story of Jacob.

2. Are these twin boys alike?............... What physical differences?..

3. What differences do you see in their interests? What is Jacob interested in?.......................
.... Esau?..

4. What trait in Esau (chapter 25) would make him less promising than Jacob for carrying out world plans?..

Chapter 27:1—28:9

5. What part does Rebekah play in Jacob's deceit of his father?..

6. Is Jacob ready to be a world leader when he leaves home?.. Why or why not?..

Chapters 29 and 30

7. How does Laban give Jacob a taste of his own trickery? ....

8. Name the sons of Jacob.

9. How does Jacob become rich at Laban's expense?..

10. *Optional:* Sketch the family tree of Jacob showing the line from Terah, his great-grand-father, and including his uncle Laban and his family.

Can you think of any reason why there was so much intermarriage within the family? How important are similar religious beliefs and cultural backgrounds in marriage?

JACOB LEARNS TO KNOW GOD

If you were promised the one thing you wanted most, what would you choose? Would you have wanted the same thing five years ago? Will you want it five years from now?

1. Study chapter 28. *Jacob's introduction to God in Bethel*
   (1) How did God introduce Himself to Jacob?...
   ....
   (2) Why was Jacob afraid?..
   (3) What did God promise Jacob?..
   (4) What did Jacob ask God for?...
       (Is prayer just asking God for things?)
   (5) What did Jacob promise God?..

2. Study chapter 32. *God's Conquest of Jacob at Penuel*
   (1) About how much later is this? (31:41)..
   (2) What did Jacob ask God for?...
   (3) How long did the "wrestling" continue?..
   (4) What change was made in Jacob's name?........................... Why?......................
   ....
   (5) Jacob won by clinging to God. (32:26) How does this differ from his usual method of getting what he wanted?...

3. Study chapter 35. *Jacob's Communion with God at Bethel*
   (1) Why did God ask Jacob to return to Bethel?..
   (2) Who went with him this time?...
   (3) What did Jacob ask God for this time?..
   (4) Which of his three prayers was most likely to please God?................................
   (5) Why?...
   (6) What did God promise Jacob?..
   ....

4. What sort of things did Jacob want from life at this time that he would have scorned as a younger man?...

5. What has he learned about God that he did not know in chapter 28?.......................
   ....

6. Would you trust Jacob now as a leader of the world?.................... Why?...............
   ....

JOSEPH, A PRINCE IN A STRANGE LAND

Read Genesis 37—50 for the familiar story of Joseph.

1. List the steps by which Joseph began as a dreamer and became ruler of Egypt. List also those steps by which his family got to Egypt. Did Joseph see in it all the plan of God for his life? Why?

----

2. Attempt to do a creative job by working with the story of Joseph in any *one* of the following ways which most appeals to you. Let your imagination work!

    (1) Write out the story of Joseph as you would tell it to a ten-year-old boy or girl, using such main divisions as the following:

    a. Joseph as a spoiled boy in Canaan.
    b. Joseph as a prisoner in Egypt.
    c. Joseph as an interpreter of dreams.
    d. Joseph as a ruler in Egypt.
    e. Joseph as a forgiving brother.

    (2) Make an outline of a play about Joseph, using the suggested headings above as titles of your scenes, or selecting three or four main events in his life which you think important and interesting. List your characters; describe your stage setting briefly; and list the events that should take place on the stage in each scene.

    (3) Try a radio script of the story. This would require your telling the story as a whole and dramatizing only those few scenes that would go well on radio.

    (4) Write a character sketch of Joseph, covering such points as the following:

    a. Was being a "pet" an advantage or a disadvantage to Joseph?
    b. What qualities helped him to become an overseer in Potiphar's house?
    c. What qualities in Joseph made Pharaoh choose him as ruler in Egypt?
    d. Do you approve of his treatment of his brothers at the end? Why?

GENESIS AS A WHOLE (A Review Lesson)

What does Genesis say to you?

1. Attempt to show how much space in the book of Genesis is given to each of the five or six main characters in the book by indicating in some way on the line below (which represents the 50 chapters of Genesis) where each entered the story and where he left it.

   1   10   20   30   40   **50**

2. Study the four great patriarchs of the Hebrew nation: Abraham, Isaac, Jacob, and Joseph. Is there any one mark of greatness that is characteristic of them all?.................................

3. Could you say that the *faith* of Abraham gave these men their religion as truly as the faith of Columbus gave us America and the faith of Edison gave us electricity?............................. What other great discoveries or great achievements have come to us through the faith of one man? List two or three that occur to you...

4. When Jacob was on his deathbed, what did he say God had done for him? (48:15, 16)..........

   What phrases in Jacob's blessing of Judah show that he is chosen for the "Covenant son"?

   How did Jacob explain Joseph's success in life? (49:23-26) ....

5. How did Joseph's last interview with his brothers reveal again his faith in God? (50:15-26)

6. How do you explain the success of this family up to this point?..

   Do you think the nation they are founding will remember these men?............................

Suppose you were a Hebrew boy or girl living in Egypt 350 years after Jacob's family moved down, under the conditions portrayed in Exodus1:1-14. What things in the book of Genesis would be most important to you?

The Beginning of the Hebrew Nation

THE NEED FOR A LEADER

Read Exodus 1 and 2.

1. Make a list of phrases which show the mistreatment of this people by the Egyptians.

2. How long had it been since Joseph brought his family down to Egypt? (Exodus 12:40)

3. How many had come to Egypt? (Exodus 1:5)

   How many were there now? (Exodus 12:37)

4. What change had taken place in the ruling family of Egypt?

5. What had caused the change in the ruler's attitude toward the Israelites?

6. List the specific steps he took to "purge" Egypt of this objectionable people.

   (1:11)

   (1:15, 16)

   (1:22)

7. Study chapter 2 for the remarkable way in which a leader for this persecuted people managed to survive through such widespread oppression.

   (1) Imagine for yourself his babyhood in his own home.

   (2) Imagine his boyhood and education at the court of Pharaoh.

8. Do you find any indication that he was sympathetic with the oppressed Hebrews?

9. How did he identify himself with their cause against the king?

10. What qualities of leadership did he show at this point?

11. What weakness do you see in him that would hinder his success as a leader?

THE CALL OF MOSES

Do you believe God has a plan for your life? How can you learn what it is? How did Moses learn?

Read Exodus 3—6.

1. *Moses' First Vision of God* (Exodus 3:1—4:17)
   (1) List the phrases by which God introduces Himself to Moses. (3:6)

   ....

   ....

   (2) Does God know the trouble the Israelites are in? List the phrases that show this. (3:7-9)

   ....

   ....

   ....

   (3) What did He promise to do for them?
   (3:10) ....
   (3:12) ....
   (3:17) ....
   (4) List the objections Moses raised to God's plan, and God's answer to each.

MOSES' OBJECTIONS	GOD'S ANSWERS
(4:1)	....
(4:10)	....
(4:13)	....

2. *Moses' Second Vision of God* (5:22—6:9)
   List the phrases by which God tries to convince Moses, using the following verb forms (this is a form of the same covenant which we found in Genesis):

I AM ...., ..., ...
I HAVE ....

....

I WILL ....

....

....

....

How far back in history does this "covenant" take us? How far forward?
Do you think God still appears to men in visions? What other ways has He of talking to us?

THE TEN PLAGUES

Can the suffering caused by World War II teach us anything? What? Was God on one "side" in the struggle between Israel and Egypt? Why do you think so?

Read Exodus 7—12.

1. Make a table showing the 10 plagues and the effect of each on Pharaoh.

PLAGUE	EFFECT ON PHARAOH
(1)	(1)
(2)	(2)
(3)	(3)
(4)	(4)
(5)	(5)
(6)	(6)
(7)	(7)
(8)	(8)
(9)	(9)
(10)	(10)

2. What is happening to Pharaoh? Is he responsible for the "hardening of his heart"?

Note the plague at which it is first definitely said that God hardened Pharaoh's heart

3. Look for the word "know" through chapters 7—12. How many times does it occur?

List some of the things that the people will *know* because of the plagues.

4. Why did not Pharaoh learn the same things the Israelites learned?

5. What would you say was the purpose of the plagues?

THE GREAT FEAST OF THE PASSOVER

Why and how do we celebrate the Fourth of July? How is it like or unlike the Jewish Passover? "History was born on the night when the children of Israel went out of Egypt."

Read Exodus 12.

1. The name PASSOVER was given to the festival because (12:12, 13):

....

2. The date: the.................month (Jewish month *Nisan,* our *March* or *April*), the.................
   day. (12:3-6)

3. The animal:...
   Its qualifications:........................., ..., ...(12:5)
   Its preparation:........................., ..., ...(12:8)

4. The people's preparation:........................., ..., ...(12:11)

5. The unleavened bread was eaten for.............days.

6. The blood of the animal was put in three places on the door:.................................... ....

....

7. As a part of the celebration of the festival, when the feast was over the youngest boy always
   asked the question (12:26):...

   And the oldest man present would always answer (12:27):...

....

8. What would be the values of such a holiday to a Jewish boy or girl living in the Promised
   Land a hundred years later? What would it mean to them or remind them of?.................

....

   What meaning do Christians like to see in the Passover ·Lamb?

9. What was the Hebrews' part in winning their freedom?..

....

   Could they have retarded or prevented it?.............How?...

....

A THREE MONTHS' TREK THROUGH THE WILDERNESS

It was a big undertaking to get the people out of slavery; it was a bigger undertaking to get the slavery out of the people. Why?

Read quickly Exodus 12—19.

1. Describe in a sentence or two the important experience that occurred at each of the following places on the journey from Egypt to Mt. Sinai:

    (1) Marah (15:23-26) ____

    ____

    (2) Elim (15:27) ____

    ____

    (3) Wilderness of Sin (Chapter 16) _________________________________

    ____

    (4) Rephidim (17:1-16) ____

    ____

    (5) Mt. Sinai____

    ____

2. Locate these places on Map III and draw a line showing the route of the journey from Goshen in Egypt to Mt. Sinai.

3. Locate the Promised Land.

4. Observe a shorter route from Egypt to Canaan which they might have taken. Could it be that they were not ready to go into the Promised Land until they knew God better? Keep this in mind in your further study.

5. Think through the events that happened to the people on this trip.

    Which place do you think they will remember most?_________________________

    Why?____

6. Remember the promises of God in 6:1-9. Would you say that God is making good His promises?___________ What evidence can you find for your answer?_______________

    ____

    ____

THE WILDERNESS JOURNEY: PLACES THAT TALK

On the map below trace the journey of the Israelites from Goshen to Sinai. Be sure to label all natural boundaries, such as bodies of water, and put on your map the places mentioned on Guide Sheet 18.

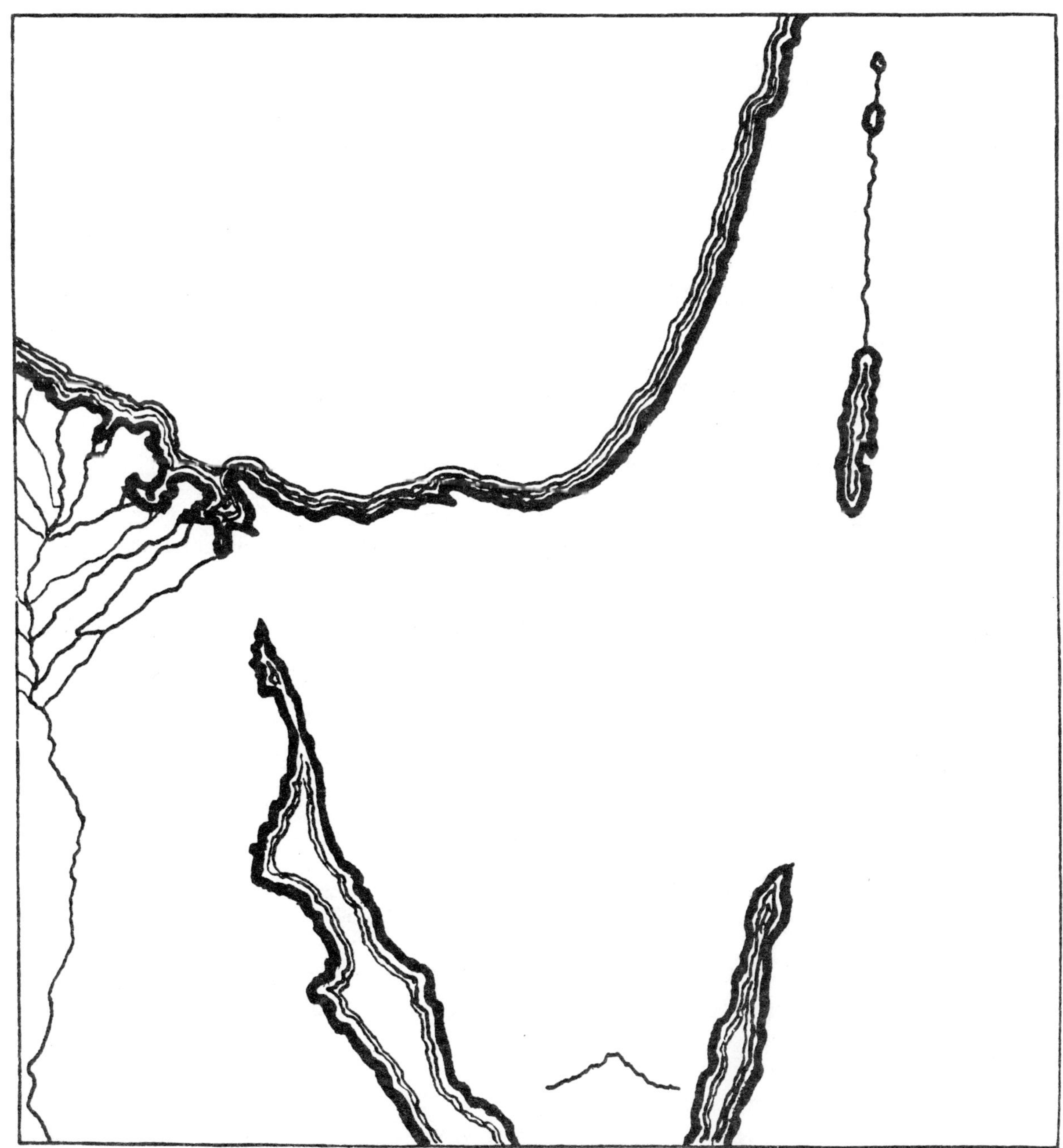

Map III   *The Wilderness Journey*

A NATION IN PARTNERSHIP WITH GOD

Have you ever made a solemn pledge to God or to some friend? How is a pledge like or unlike a covenant?

Read Exodus 19—24.

1. List the promises God made to Israel. (19:4-6)

   ____

   ____

2. Quote the response of the people to Jehovah. (19:8)

   ____

3. How is this covenant unlike the one in Exodus 6:1-9?

   ____

4. What rules were made to make the people realize the holiness of God?
   (Exodus 19:12-14) ____

5. How did God show the people that He was on the Mount? (19:16-19)

   ____

6. Memorize the Ten Commandments. The people's share of the Covenant was their promise to obey these commands.

7. Exodus 20:22—23:19 is called "The Book of the Covenant." List three of these laws that interest you most, summarizing in a few words and giving references.

   (1) ____
   (2) ____
   (3) ____

8. Read 24:1-8 for the story of the signing of the covenant.
   What animals were killed for the sacrifice? ___________________________
   In what two ways did Moses use the blood of the animals?
   (1) _______________________________ (2) ______________________________
   It was customary to sprinkle a drop of blood on each party to a contract.

9. Quote the pledge of the people to God. (24:3) _____________________________

   ____

10. Do you suppose the covenant would be easy to keep? _________What would the effort mean
    to them? ____

A BROKEN PROMISE

Have you ever failed to keep a promise? What did it cost you? Did Israel fail to keep one? Why? How?

1. Read Exodus 24:12-18 for the conditions of Moses' first stay on Mt. Sinai with God. Companion... Length of stay... Who was left in charge of the people?..........................and...

2. Read Exodus 32—34. Do you consider Aaron or the people to blame for the golden calf? Prove your point briefly... ....

3. Did Aaron consider the golden calf a substitute for God or a means of worshipping God? Cite references to prove your point... ....

   Why could the people not worship God in that way?...

4. Do you admire Aaron's attitude when accused by Moses?... Why, or why not?...

5. How were the people punished?... ....

6. What new ideas of God came to Moses from this experience?
   (1) Under what conditions does God become angry? (33:1-5)
   ....

   (2) What is the effect of prayer on God? (33:13-17)
   ....

   (3) Can man ever completely know God? (33:19-23)
   ....

   (4) What new interpretation of the word "Jehovah" or "Lord" is given? (34: 6, 7)..........
   ....

   (5) What is man's obligation to God if God is to be enabled to keep His covenant promises? (34:10-17)...

7. How is this experience tied up with those previous covenants?
   (1) The covenant in Egypt (6:1-9)...
   (2) The covenant at Sinai (19:1-6)...

THE TABERNACLE—A HOUSE OF WORSHIP

Read Exodus 25—31; 35—40.

Note that chapters 25—31 contain instructions for the building as given to Moses on the Mount and that 35—40 contain the carrying out of these instructions by the people.

PLAN OF THE TABERNACLE:

1. Brazen altar.
2. Laver.
3. Table of showbread.
4. Candlestick.
5. Altar of incense.
6. Mercy Seat and Ark of the Covenant.

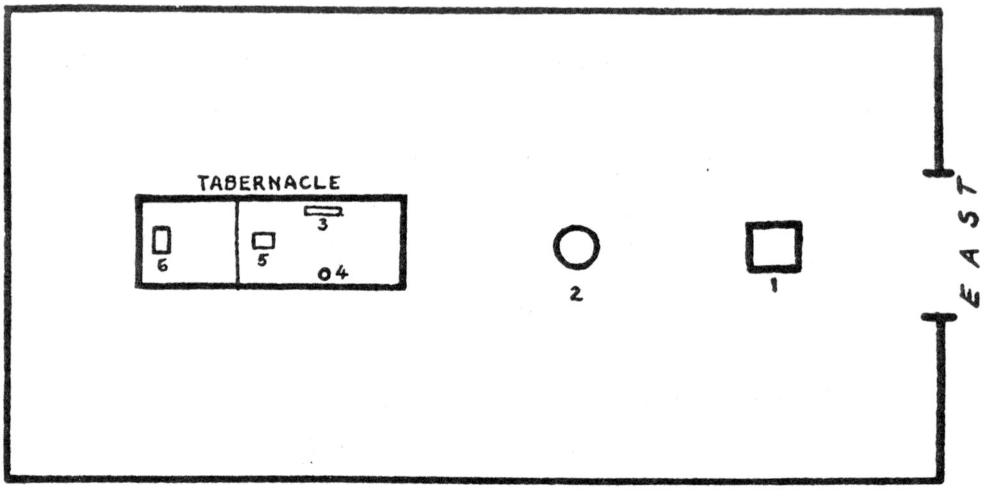

What does the word "Tabernacle" mean?..

1. How was this Tabernacle to be financed? (35:4-9)..
    Compare with modern methods.

2. List the gifts that could be used. (35:4-9)

3. What kind of response did the people make? (35:20-29; 36:2-7)

    (The amount in our money has been estimated at from $400,000 to $1,250,000.)

4. What two men were put in charge of the work? (36:1)..**and**
    .... What requirements were made of them?..

5. When was the Tabernacle completed? (40:17)...

6. How did the people know that God was pleased with their work?

What ideals do you discover here for modern church buildings?

THE BOOK OF EXODUS (A Review Lesson)

1. Block out the book geographically, showing which chapters occur in each place.

        EGYPT   **WILDERNESS**   **SINAI**

1____40

2. Discover if possible the lapse of time in each section and indicate on the above sketch. (Exodus 19:1; 40:17)

3. Think of this whole experience as a means of learning about God. What have the people learned in the short time since they left Sinai? List the greatest experiences they have had and what each experience taught them about God or about themselves.

       (1) The experiences   Lessons about God

       (2) The experiences   Lessons about themselves as a nation

4. Express the purpose or principal idea of Exodus in a sentence.

     Can you see any way in which each lesson in Exodus supports the purpose you have stated? Write this down.

Sheet 14____

Sheet 15____

Sheet 16____

Sheet 17____

Sheet 18____

Sheet 19____

Sheet 20____

Sheet 21____

The Hebrew Manual of Worship

ARE YOU A RELIGIOUS PERSON?

(This unit on Leviticus may be considered optional. Its primary purpose is to direct the student to an introductory study of some of the Hebrew forms of worship, and to some critical thinking about worship on his own account.)

1. Have you ever felt that God was actually with you? Try to recall one occasion when the feeling of God's presence was particularly vivid.

2. On what kind of occasion do people feel the need for God?

3. On what kind of occasion do people feel far away from God?

4. How can you explain the fact that people do find it necessary to know God?

5. List several ways we have of knowing God.

6. How would you define prayer?

7. Write down several different reasons for praying.

8. What are some other ways we have of worshipping God besides prayer?

9. Glance through the book of Leviticus to see what ways of worship the Hebrews had. You may be very sure that their ways will be different from our own. List all the methods of worship you can find and try to explain briefly what each could have meant to them. If you cannot understand the meaning and purpose, hold these things in mind for more intensive study of the book and then return to this sheet.

WHY HAVE SPECIAL DAYS OF WORSHIP?

1. Make a list of all the holidays we celebrate, and write down beside each the idea of the event we are celebrating.

....

....

....

....

....

Put a check mark beside the ones which you would consider in any sense *religious* holidays.

2. What Jewish holiday have you already studied in Exodus 12 and 13?

....

3. In what sense may this event be called "the birth of a nation"?

....

4. Which one of our holidays is most like it in its purpose?..

5. Read Leviticus 23, and list the "holy convocations" or "feasts" which the Hebrews celebrated each year. Try to discover from your Bible or from a good commentary or Bible dictionary the meaning or purpose of each holiday and the time of year of each.

HOLIDAY	MEANING	SEASON

6. Notice that these days were celebrated by feasting or by sacrifices and offerings to God, or both. What would you say seems to be the purpose of making offerings to God?........................

....

....

DOES IT COST TO DO WRONG?

1. One of the reasons the Hebrews had for bringing offerings to God was a consciousness that they had done wrong. Read Leviticus 4 and 5 for an account of the "sin offering" and the "trespass offering."

   (1) If a priest had done some wrong and felt guilty in God's sight, how could he show his sorrow and repentance?...

   ....

   (2) How could a ruler show his repentance?...

   ....

   (3) How could one of the common people?...

   ....

   (4) Why was it more serious for a ruler to sin than for one of the people?.............................

   ....

   (5) Why most serious of all for a priest?...

   (6) If a man had stolen something from someone else, what must he do before he could find satisfaction in worship? (Leviticus 5:14-16)

   ....

2. Study Leviticus 16 for an account of the DAY OF ATONEMENT. This is the most solemn day in the whole year for the Hebrew nation.

   (1) Notice that three animals are used for this ceremony of cleansing. List the three and what is done to each.

   a. ....

   b. ....

   c. ....

   (2) How does this study of the DAY OF ATONEMENT help you to understand what Christians mean when they speak of Jesus Christ as "making atonement for" our sins?

   ....

   (3) Is it true that one person may suffer for the sins of another?...

3. What conclusions can you draw about the cost of wrongdoing?...

   ....

   ....

DOES WORSHIP REALLY MAKE ANY DIFFERENCE?

1. What happens to people when they really worship God? Someone has said that "to worship well is to live well." Have you ever felt that you were different in any way after an experience of worship? Or have you known other people who have been changed by worship? Describe this experience briefly.

    ----

2. Can an experience of God change your way of thinking about things? Help you to feel more appreciative of another race? Help you to see the foolishness of superstitious ideas like the "bad luck" we associate with black cats and broken mirrors? Make you more considerate of other people? Write a brief paragraph explaining what effect a strong conviction of the reality of God will have on one of these things.

    ----

3. Read Leviticus 19 for some of the ways in which the lives of the Hebrew people will be affected if they really worship God. Jot down some of the commandments that interest you: for example, 19:9, 10; 19:11, 12; 19:16; etc.

    ----

4. Note the repeated use of the words, "I am the Lord." Can you think of any reason for this? What have they learned by now of the character of their God? Is a person affected at all by the character of the person he worships?

    ----

5. Attempt to summarize in a paragraph what you consider the true meaning of worship and what particular features of Hebrew worship seem most meaningful to you. (Use another sheet of paper if necessary.)

The Wandering in the Wilderness

THE ISRAELITES ARE A GREAT ARMY

1. Glance through Numbers 1. What occurs to you as the explanation of the name of this book?..
Thumb through the book for another chapter in which this same thing happens again..........

2. After a study of chapters 2 and 3, sketch a drawing of the camp of the Israelites, locating the twelve tribes of Israel as directed in chapter 2, and the groups of Levites as directed in chapter 3. Be careful to locate the Levites between the Tabernacle and the tribes. Can you think of any reason for this arrangement?

3. What is the meaning of the central location of the Tabernacle?

----

4. Read Numbers 9 and 10. Try to picture the great procession of Israelites as they left Mt. Sinai on their march toward the Promised Land.

   (1) Can you think of any reason for celebrating the Passover before starting out on this difficult journey?

   ----

   (2) What part did each of the following play on the journey?
   a. The cloud..
   b. The pillar of fire...
   c. The trumpets of silver...
   d. "Rise up, Lord, and let thine enemies be scattered; and let them that hate thee flee before thee."

   ----

   e. "Return, O Lord, unto the many thousands of Israel."

What reason can you think of for the discipline and formality of organization at this stage of Hebrew development?

THE ISRAELITES LEARN SLOWLY

1. Read Numbers 11 and 12. List the things that any of the Israelites did which show dissatisfaction, or a lack of faith in God; and indicate how God dealt with each individual.

    (1) The people..

    (2) Moses..

    (3) Miriam and Aaron...

2. Were any of these complaints the same as those made during their journey in the wilderness in the book of Exodus? Which?

    ----

3. Is God any more severe in His treatment of the people than He was in Exodus? Compare their cries for food and God's answers.

    ----

4. Can you account for this? Why should God expect more of the people now than He did at that time?

    ----

5. Read Numbers 13 and 14. Where did this episode take place?...............................
    Look up on a map to see how close the people were to the end of their journey to the Promised Land.

6. What sort of things did the people want the spies to find out about the land that was to be their new home?..

7. In the report of the 12 spies, what things did they tell about the land that made the people want to go into the land God had promised them?

    ----

8. What in the report made them afraid to go?..

9. What two men were convinced that God would help them conquer the land?....................
    ....and..

10. How do you account for the fear of the people? (This is what slavery can do.)...................

11. Think through the fact that the people were to undergo forty years of wandering. Should this be explained merely as a punishment of the people for their unfaithfulness, or can it be that the people who had been born in slavery were unable to muster enough courage for such a venture? Try to justify your answer.

BUT THE ISRAELITES ARE STILL HARD TO TEACH

Read Numbers 15—21.

1. Can you explain the severe punishment for breaking the Sabbath?
   (15:32-36) ____

2. Read Numbers 16 carefully. What complaint was made against Moses and Aaron?
   ____
   By whom? ____
   What happened to them? ____

3. How did God establish forever in the minds of the people the right of Aaron and his sons to be priests? (Chapter 17)
   ____
   How was the evidence of this to be preserved? ____

4. Study Numbers 20. What did Moses do that kept him from going into the Promised Land?
   ____
   What actually was the sin? (Note vs. 10 and vs. 12)
   ____
   Were the people at all to blame for his sin?
   ____
   Was his punishment too severe? ________Explain ________________________
   ____

5. What was the sin of the people that resulted in the making of a serpent of brass? (21:4-9)
   ____
   How did God use this to teach the people faith?
   ____
   How did Jesus use this incident in John 3:14?
   ____

6. What impression of the people have you received from these chapters?
   ____

7. What seems to be the great purpose of God through these chapters?
   ____

NUMBERS—A BOOK OF TRAVEL

1. Describe in a sentence or two the event associated with each of the following places:

   (1) Mt. Sinai (the event in Numbers) ....

   ....

   (2) Taberah (11:1-3) ....

   ....

   (3) Kibroth-hattaavah (11:4-34) ....

   ....

   (4) Hazeroth (11:35—12:15) ....

   ....

   (5) Kadesh (13, 14, 20:1) ....

   ....

   ....

   (6) Meribah (20:2-13) ....

   ....

   ....

   (7) Mt. Hor (20:22-29) ....

   ....

   ....

   (8) Moab (Chapters 22—36) ....

   ....

   ....

2. Locate these places on your map of the book of Exodus. (Map III) This will now show the complete journey of the Israelites from Egypt to the edge of the Promised Land.

What changes in the attitude of the people occurred as an accompaniment of these geographic changes? Why are these changes in attitude and in geography important for the Hebrews?

THE BOOK OF NUMBERS (A Review Lesson)

Choose one of the following:

1. Attempt to portray the book of Numbers with a chart or diagram of some kind. One of the following suggestions may prove helpful:

   (1) Choose a descriptive subtitle for the book, such as "God's Discipline of the People" or "The Preparation of the People for the Promised Land" and show the events in the book that are definitely related to that idea.

   (2) Center the book around the historic title of "Numbers," arranging the material so as to show the reasonableness of the title.

   (3) Center the book around its mountains.

   (4) Let the book portray the great genius of Moses as a leader.

   (5) Perhaps the book suggests to you a great "Theocracy" or God-centered nation. Relate each of its parts to that conception.

2. If you do not care to make a chart or diagram of the book, you may prefer to substitute a study of one of the problems raised by the book. Choose one problem that interests you. Think it through. Read as widely as possible. Consult other people whose judgment you trust. Then write an essay of two or three pages presenting a solution to the problem that satisfies you, and your reasons for arriving at your conclusions.

   Some of the problems raised on your guide sheets may suggest a topic to you.

3. Write an essay of two or three pages on some particular aspect of Moses. This can be a means of reviewing his whole career. Do not attempt to tell everything you know about him. Choose one phase of his life or his character; make a single statement that expresses the thing about him that most interests you, and let your essay be a development or a proof of that single statement.

   Some of the following questions may prove suggestive:

   (1) What do you think is the greatest thing Moses did?

   (2) What would you say were his most valuable contributions to your world?

   (3) What were the most valuable contributions he made to his own nation?

   (4) What do you think was the reason for his greatness? Was it heredity? Environment? Had it anything to do with God?

   (5) Were the prayers of Moses disrespectful?

   (6) If Moses was truly described as "meek," what would you say meekness is?

   (7) What constitutes true greatness? Was Moses great by your definition?

The Farewell Address of Moses

MOSES' LAST ATTEMPT TO HELP THE PEOPLE KNOW GOD

Read Deuteronomy 1—4.

The location...

The date (how long after leaving Egypt).........................

The teacher...The pupils...
(Were these the same Israelites who had left Egypt?)

The problem: See whether you can think through some of the changes that would take place in the lives of the people when they began to settle in Canaan.

Their leader ....

Their homes ....

Their occupations ....

Their food..

(In answering these questions, recall that the nomadic life of the past forty years was over and they were about to become a settled people. Look up in some reference book enough information to satisfy your curiosity about life in Canaan at that time.)

Deuteronomy is Moses' attempt to meet the problem. It is a series of addresses to the people in which he seems to be answering certain great questions, the first of which is:

HOW CAN WE KNOW THERE REALLY IS A GOD?

Have you ever been in doubt of God? Does He ever seem unreal or far away? How do you explain this?

1. Read Deuteronomy 1-3. These chapters contain a summary of the history of the Israelites. How did Moses tell this story so that it would prove to the Israelites that there was a God?

   ....

2. Read chapter 4 two or three times. List every phrase that shows anything about the nature or character of their God.

   ....

   ....

   ....

   ....

Would you be convinced that there was a God if these exciting events had happened to you or to your family? In what ways can history show us something about the character of God?

[43]

WHAT DIFFERENCE DOES GOD MAKE?

Would your life be any different if there were no such God as Moses was talking about? Would it be different if you just believed that there were no such God?

1. Can you think of any reason for the Israelites to love God? ....

2. Is Moses justified in summing up the laws of God (the Ten Commandments) in one great commandment as he did in Deuteronomy 6:4, 5? ....

   It was St. Augustine of the fourth century A.D. (some 1600-1800 years later than Moses) who said, "Love God and do as you please." Do you think this would work as a rule of life? Why or why not? ....

3. Did the Israelites deserve any credit for God's having chosen them for special care and protection? See what Moses told them:
   (1) Deuteronomy 7:7, "Not . . . because ye were..."
   (2) Deuteronomy 9:4, 5, "Not for thy..."
   (3) Deuteronomy 7:8, "But because..."

4. What suggestions did Moses give the Israelites to make sure that this commandment would always be uppermost in their hearts? (6:6-9) ....

5. What suggestion did Moses make to be sure that the children of later generations would be educated in this same principle of love? (6:20-24) ....

6. Memorize Deuteronomy 6:4, 5. Can you recall the circumstances under which Jesus quoted these verses many hundreds of years later? ....

WHAT HAS LOVE TO DO WITH LIFE?

Why be good? Does what you really believe affect the way you live? Why?

1. The Hebrews believed that if they were to love God with all their heart, soul, and might, there were certain things they could not do.

    (1) What about blood? (Ch. 12)

    (2) How serious is idolatry? (Ch. 13)

    (3) What about mutilating their bodies? (14:1, 2)

    (4) What about the kind of food they might eat? (14:3-21)

2. There are certain rules of the economic life that will follow if the people love God.

    (1) About real estate (19:14)

    (2) Hunting laws (22:6, 7)

    (3) Lost property (22:1-3)

    (4) Moneylending (23:19)

    (5) Weights and measures (25:13-16)

3. They must consider the privileges and property of other people.

    (1) Railings around roofs of houses (22:8)

    (2) Gleaning in the fields (24:19-22)

    (3) Taking other people's grapes, etc. (23:24, 25)

4. If the people are to love God, there are certain forms of worship they will want to observe. Explain the following briefly:

    (1) The tithe (14:22, 28)

    (2) The Sabbatical year (Ch. 15)

    (3) Religious festivals (Ch. 16)

5. In what sense is 14:1a the keynote of this whole section of the book?

DOES IT REALLY PAY TO BE GOOD? WHAT WILL BE THE RESULTS OF EVIL?

1. Read Deuteronomy 8 carefully. How has God treated the Israelites in the past? (8:2-4)

2. Why has He allowed them to suffer at all? (8:2-5)

3. What good things does He promise them? (8:7-10)

4. What danger does He foresee in the midst of such prosperity? (8:11-18)

5. What warning does He give? (8:19, 20)

6. Read carefully Deuteronomy 10:12-22; 11:8-17; 11:26-28; and chapter 28. These passages seem to show that blessings and prosperity are a natural result of obedience to God's law, and that calamity and poverty are a result of disobedience. Have you found this to be true in your experience with people? Discuss.

7. Is it difficult and unnatural to be good? List the expressions in chapter 30 that seem to show that Moses considers obedience to God's law as a natural thing and essential to real living.

From your own experience do you find that wrongdoing costs more than it is worth or not? Do you consider sin a worth-while investment? Do you think that good people are happy? Why?

[46]

The Settlement of the Promised Land

THE MIRACULOUS ENTRANCE INTO THE PROMISED LAND

Joshua has been called "The Sir Galahad of the Old Testament."

1. Read Joshua 1—5. What brief command is repeated 3 or 4 times in Joshua 1?

2. List some of the promises God made to Joshua in this chapter.

3. Upon what two things does Joshua's success depend?
   (1) ....(1:8)
   (2) ....(1:9)
   Of Sir Galahad it is said: "His strength was as the strength of ten because his heart was pure."

4. Study the experiences of the two spies. (Chapter 2) What did Rahab tell them about the reputation of Israel?

   Did that help?...............How?...............
   What bargain did she make with them?...............

   What report did they bring back from Jericho?...............

5. Get a clear mental picture of the miracle of the Jordan River (Chapters 3 and 4)
   The condition of the river (3:15)...............
   What did the priests do that kept the people from being afraid?

   How did the memorial stones represent ALL the people?

6. Explain briefly the importance of each of the four things that occurred after the crossing of the river.
   (1) Circumcision ....
   (2) Passover...............
   (3) Ceasing of the manna...............
   (4) Vision of angel with sword...............

THE CAPTURE OF FOREIGN CITIES

Have you ever known a football team from a very small high school to be victorious over a team from a large school? How did you explain it?

Read Joshua 6—9.

1. Tell the story of the fall of Jericho as a man from the tribe of Reuben might have told it to his young son on his return home across the Jordan. (Use another sheet of paper)

2. Read about the failure to capture the second city, Ai.

    (1) What did the Hebrews expect to happen?...

    (2) What actually happened?...

    (3) Whose fault was it?...

    (4) What had he kept that should have been God's?..

    (5) Do you consider his punishment too severe?.................Explain..................................

    ....

3. By what trick did the people of Gibeon seek to save their lives? Look up Gibeon on a map to see how close it was to Gilgal and then read 9:3-13.

    ....

    ....

    (1) How would you costume and make up the Gibeonites if you were putting on a dramatic skit of "The Tricky Gibeonites"?

    ....

    ....

    (2) Why would not Joshua break his covenant with them when he found they had deceived him?

    ....

    (3) Do you think he was right?.................Why?..

    ....

4. How would the Israelites explain these successes and near-failures?

    (1) Jericho..

    (2) Ai...

    (3) Gibeon..

THE SETTLING OF THE PROMISED LAND

Fill in the map below as one of the Israelites might have done for his son, to show him more clearly what adventures he had been engaging in during the conquest and division of the land.

Show the exciting battles, the unusual experiences. An Israelite would have prized particularly the events in which God worked miracles.

He would have pointed out where each of the twelve tribes finally settled.

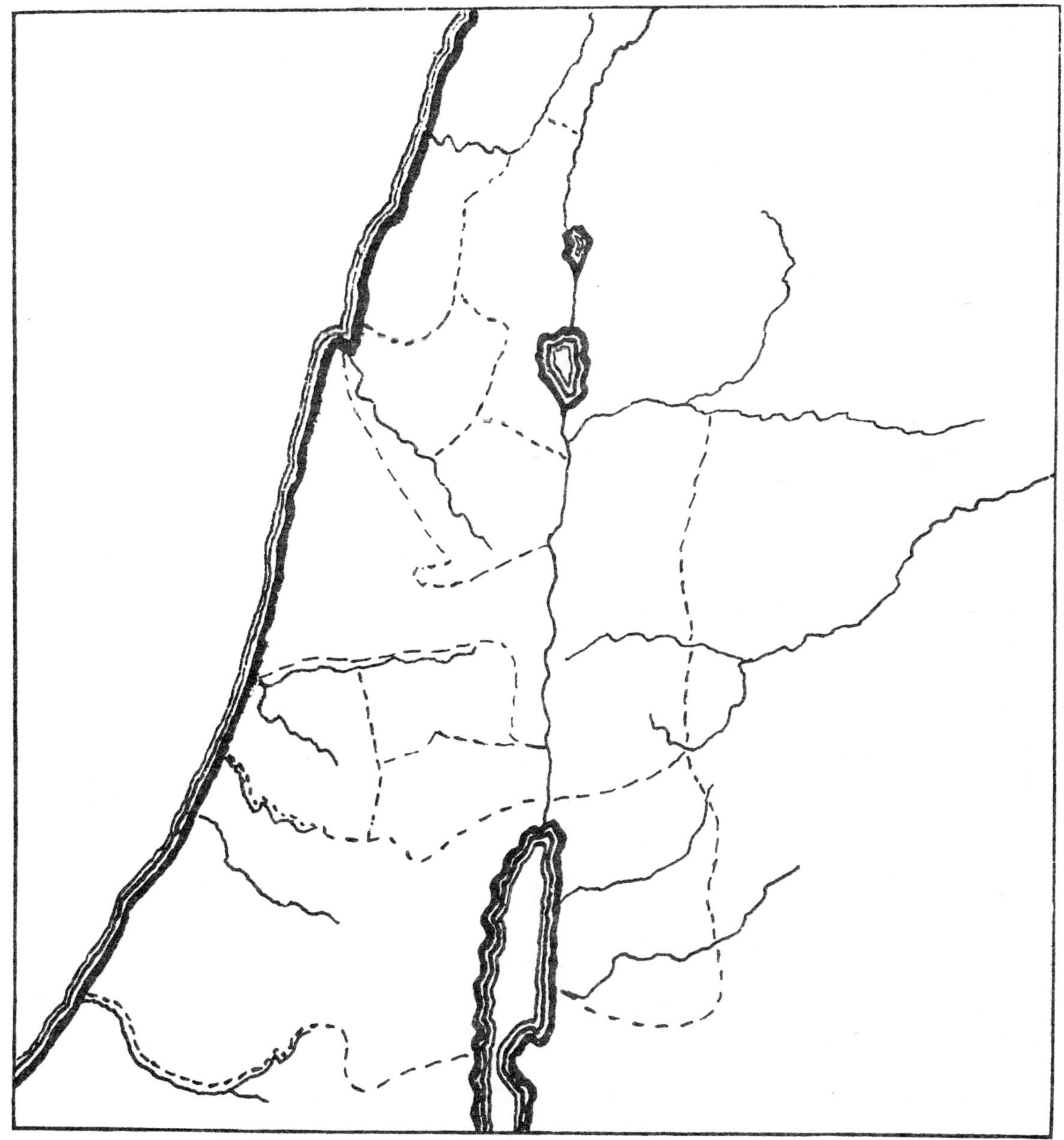

MAP IV   *The Settling of the Promised Land*

JOSHUA'S FAREWELL ADDRESSES

I. TO THE LEADERS OF THE PEOPLE (Chapter 23)

1. List the officers to whom he spoke ....

....

2. What warnings did he give them? ....

....

3. How did he explain their success up to this time? (23:3) ....

....

4. What promises did he make to them? ....

....

II. TO THE PEOPLE THEMSELVES (Chapter 24)

1. List several important individuals Joshua mentioned in reviewing their history.

....

2. What miraculous events in their history did he recall?

....

....

3. What choice did he give them?

Either ....

Or ....

"But as for me and my house, ..."

Did his "we will" have behind it a long history of "we have" so far as Joshua was concerned?

4. How many times did Joshua make the people repeat their pledge of allegiance to God before he was satisfied? ....

5. What visible witness of their pledge did he set up? ....

Where? .... Was this a good idea? .... Why? ....

....

What do you think was the biggest thing Joshua did for the Hebrews?

The Dark Ages of Israel

THE DARK AGES

Notice what happens when everyone does exactly as he pleases.

1. Glance through Judges 1. Make a note of the foreign people who had not been driven completely out of Canaan.
   _________________________   _________________________   _________________________

2. Note what happened to the Israelites after the death of Joshua. (2:10)
   ____

3. Note the situation which resulted from the contact with the foreign people. (2:11-23)
   ____
   Their punishment (2:14, 15)____
   Observe that this happened over and over again in this period of the Judges.

4. What kind of leaders were the "judges"? How do they differ from judges as we know them? (2:16-18) ____

5. There were 13 of these judges. Skim through the book for their names, the length of their rule, the foreign nation which had oppressed the Israelites, and the length of the oppression. (The Bible does not give all the suggested details about each oppression.)

	REF.	OPPRESSOR	TIME	JUDGE	LENGTH OF RULE
(1)	3:8 ff.	Mesopotamia	8 years	Othniel	40 years
(2)	3:12ff.				
(3)	3:31ff.				
(4)	4:2 ff.				
(5)	6:1 ff.				
(6)	9:1 ff.				
(7)	10:1 ff.				
(8)	10:3 ff.				
(9)	10:7 ff.				
(10)	12:8 ff.				
(11)	12:11ff.				
(12)	12:13ff.				
(13)	13:1 ff.				

HEROES AND HEROINES

How do you account for the fact that out of great extremity great heroes are born?

Attempt to read as many of these hero stories as you have time for. (Judges 3—12) Many of them are familiar, but you will be interested in reading them again in their setting and seeing their place in the great stream of Hebrew history.

1. Choose *one* of the following projects for special preparation:

    (1) Select one of the Judges—Ehud, Deborah, Gideon, Jephthah—and be prepared to tell the story to the class. Look for details that will give the following information:

    a. The situation under the oppression of a foreign nation.
    b. The circumstances that caused the "judge" to come to the rescue of his people.
    c. The method of overcoming the enemy.

    (2) Plan with a small group from the class to present the story to the class dramatically. You might do this in pantomime or you might find it interesting as a radio script. The story of Jephthah would be excellent material for dramatization.

    (3) Write two letters, as follows:

    a. The letter that Deborah might have written her husband telling about her experiences as the captain of a great army. Include such things as the arguments that Barak used to get her help; the tribes that rallied to her cry; Sisera's war equipment; and the thing that turned the course of the battle.

    b. The letter that Jael might have written her husband telling of her part in the battle. Include her feelings, as you would imagine them, both before and after the deed she did.

2. On the basis of the story you worked on, be prepared to discuss in class the following questions:

    (1) What reasons do you find for calling this period "the Dark Ages"?

    (2) What did the people expect from God during these years? Was it enough? Was it too much?

    (3) Is prosperity dangerous to a nation, as Moses had warned that it might be? Illustrate from one of these stories.

    (4) How do you account for the low state of the religion of the people during this period?

SAMSON, THE PLAYBOY OF ISRAEL

1. Read the story of Samson and think through its possibilities as a play. (Judges 13—16)

2. List the characters that are essential to the story.

3. Choose three of the stories told about him which would make the best dramatic scenes, reveal his character best, and carry the story forward.

4. Think out one point you ought to make throughout the play. This should be the conclusion of the last act.

   (1) What is the tragedy of Samson's life?

   (2) What is his greatest weakness?

   (3) Can you imagine how different Samson's life could have been if he had taken his **Nazarite** vow more seriously?

   (4) What is the relation of the Nazarite vow to the rest of his life?

   (5) Do you find it mentioned anywhere in the story except before his birth?

   (6) Do you find it hinted at?

   (7) Did the strength of Samson really lie in his hair or in something the hair stood for?

5. Are you more impressed with his strength or with his weakness?

6. Was Samson deliberately cruel?

7. Was Samson a product of his times in his lack of spiritual insight?

8. Were the other members of his tribe proud of him?

9. Someone has called Samson the "playboy" of Israel. If so, what would be your definition of a playboy?

10. Samson's name means "the sunny one." He has been called a practical joker. Can you recall instances of such jokes? Were they funny?

11. Will the play about Samson be a tragedy or a comedy?

Bring to class your suggestions about the material that should be included in each of the **three** acts of a three-act play. Have in mind the climax or end of each act as something that **would** clinch the thought you have in mind.

RUTH, A FOREIGN GIRL WHO BECAME AN ISRAELITE

But the Dark Ages were not completely dark. There were some people who were loyal to God and to each other.

1. Read the book straight through for the sheer beauty and interest of the story. Now go back and list step by step the way Ruth became the great-grandmother of David.

2. Attempt to put the story in the form of a play, using some such scenes as the three suggested below:

    (1) Ruth's Sacrifice

    (2) Ruth's Service

    (3) Ruth's Romance

    For each scene that you choose, write out the following information:

    (1) The characters necessary for each.

    (2) The time and place of the action.

    (3) Description of how the stage must look.

    (4) Summary of the action of each scene and the topics of conversation.

    (5) Think of a closing speech for the end of the scene. This should make the audience wonder what will happen next, except in the last scene, where it should bring the play to a conclusion.

3. You might prefer to prepare a radio script or a moving-picture scenario.

4. You might try your hand at an original poem on the loyalty of Ruth or on some other subject suggested to you by this story.

5. Another possibility would be to prepare the story for a choral reading by the class. You might select the persons from the class who you think could read each part best, and decide which explanatory and connecting verses should be read by the chorus of voices and which verses could be omitted altogether without hurting the story.

The Rise of a Monarchy

SAMUEL, A YOUNG REFORMER

This is a good example of one way to choose your life work. Try to discover why Samuel became a reformer.

1. Read I Samuel 1—3. List the things that show the need of a reformer.

   1:13, 14 ....

   2:12-17 ....

   2:29 ....

2. Study the family of Samuel.

   (1) Father .... Mother ....

   (2) Where did they live? (1:1 and 2:11) ....

   (3) What situation in their home made Hannah's childlessness particularly hard for her
       to bear? ....

   (4) Would you say this was a religious home? .... What two indications of it do you
       find in 1:13 and 1:10, 11?

       a. ....

       b. ....

3. Explain the provisions of the Nazarite vow which Samuel's mother made for him. (See
   Numbers 6:13-20; I Samuel 1:11; and I Samuel 1:24-28)

   ....

   ....

4. Read Hannah's Song of Thanksgiving at the birth of her child. (2:1-10) Turn to Luke
   1:46-55 and read Mary's song at the birth of Jesus. Do you find any similarities?

   ....

5. Where was the Tabernacle located? ....

   Who was the priest to whom Samuel was entrusted? ....

   Who were his sons? ....

   Were these men worthy to be religious leaders of the people? (2:23-25) .... Was Eli

   to blame at all for this situation? (2:27-29) .... Why? ....

   What punishment did God threaten? ....

6. Read the story of Samuel's first vision of God. (Chapter 3)

   What was the message God gave him? ....

   What was the reward of his faithfulness in carrying out God's command? (3:19-21) ....

   ....

THE DEMAND FOR A KING

What do you think is the best kind of government?

Read I Samuel 8—11.

1. Why has the world recently turned from monarchy as a form of government? What **did** God and Samuel think of it some 3,000 years ago when the Israelites asked for a king?

    ....

    ....

2. Recall as much as you can about the government the Hebrew nation has had from the time of Abraham until now. Look up in a dictionary a definition of the two types of government they have had.

    Patriarchy: ....

    Theocracy: ....

3. What sort of leaders are necessary if a theocracy is to be successful?................................

    ....

4. Why had the period of the Judges made the Israelites dissatisfied with their form of government?..

5. What were the people's reasons for wanting a king? ....

    ....

    Did the strength of Israel depend on their being *like* or *unlike* other nations?................

6. The success of a monarchy depends on the choice of a king. Study Saul carefully to **see** whether you think he was a good choice.

    (1) Describe him physically..

    (2) What was he doing when Samuel found him?..

    (3) How did Samuel convince him that he was to be king?................................

    ....

    (4) What shows you his modesty?..

7. How was Saul accepted by the people as a whole? (10:24)................................

    By a minority group? (10:27)..

8. How did Saul measure up in his first adventure as king? (Chapter 11)................

    ....

9. List the qualities that you think will make Saul a good king................................

    ....

SAUL, THE KING WHO LOST HIS JOB

Have you ever lost a job? Why? What advice would you give a person just starting out in a new job?

Study I Samuel 9—15 for the story of Saul. Be prepared to debate the question: "Resolved that Samuel was justified in rejecting Saul as king."

1. Study such things as his heredity. (9:1, 2)
   Your first impression of him. (9:3-27; 10:20-25)
   His prowess in battle. (11:1-11)
   His generosity to his enemies. (11:13)

2. Read about his battle with the Philistines in chapter 13.
   Note the size of his army as opposed to that of the enemy.
   Note the lack of morale of the people. (Vs. 6, 7)
   Note the lack of weapons. (Vs. 19-22)
   Observe that Samuel rebuked him for making an offering himself instead of waiting for the priest. Was this wrong for a king? Why? Did Saul offer the sacrifice in order to lead the army to trust God, or to hold it together around himself? Why do you think so?

3. What do you think of Saul's oath? (14:24)
   Do you consider that his motive was good?
   In view of the tragedy of Jephthah's daughter, what do you think of this near-sacrifice of Jonathan?
   How does Saul impress you throughout this incident? Is he jealous of Jonathan?

4. Note the successes of Saul in taking care of his people. (14:47, 48)

5. How does Saul impress you in his meeting with Samuel at Gilgal? (Chapter 15)
   Would you consider him a "good sport" or did he try to shift the responsibility?
   Was Saul truly repentant? (Vs. 24-31)
   What is your definition of "repentance"? Sorrow for wrongdoing? Sorrow for being found out? Reformation, or change of heart?

6. Take one side or the other and write out the three or four points by which you intend to support your contention.

   (1) ....

   (2) ....

   (3) ....

   (4) ....

What qualities in ourselves may cause us to lose our greatest opportunities?

A SHEPHERD BOY WHO BECAME KING

What are the qualities most essential for a leader? Are our usual standards for political office high enough?

Read I Samuel 16—19.

1. What new requirement was given Samuel for picking out the second king? (16:7)............

2. List the information you can discover about David. (Chapter 16) Appearance......................

   His home town...........................His father's name...........................

   His occupation ....One of his hobbies...........................

   Experiences of his boyhood (17:34, 35)...........................

3. Read Psalms 23, 19, 8, 29. These Psalms may not have been written while David was a shepherd boy, but they seem to reflect ideas gained during that period of his life. Write down one thing from each Psalm that David apparently learned about God from his years outdoors.

   Psalm 23...........................

   Psalm 19...........................

   Psalm 8...........................

   Psalm 29...........................

4. What jobs did David have at the court of Saul? ....

5. Try to discover new things about *how* and *why* this boy killed a giant. What was his reason for being so sure of success in this?...........................

6. Why did he become popular with the people?...........................

7. Why was he unpopular with Saul?...........................

8. Think through the friendship of David and Jonathan. Which one had more to lose because of this friendship?...........................

   What are some of the marks of true friendship? List several proofs that Jonathan's was true...........................

9. Do you think David will satisfy your ideal of what a king should be? List the qualities that will make him a great king...........................

SAUL DESTROYS HIMSELF

Is a bad disposition something one inherits or are we responsible for it? Can temper be controlled? Is our success or failure in life our own fault?

1. List the attempts of Saul to get rid of David, as given in I Samuel 18 and 19.
   (1) ....(18:10, 11)
   (2) ....(18:22-29)
   (3) ....(19:1)
   (4) ....(19:9, 10)
   (5) ....(19:11-17)

2. What apparently is happening to Saul at this time? List adjectives that describe him as he appears in these stories...

   ....

3. Skim through chapters 20—31 for the stories of the downfall of Saul.
   (1) How does Jonathan help David to escape from Saul? (Chapter 20)..........................

   ....

   (Remember in these stories that Jonathan was the logical person to follow his father as king. This makes him a very amazing person.)
   (2) How does Saul's jealousy cause him to slay 85 priests? (Chapters 21, 22)....................

   ....

   (3) Why does David spare Saul's life at two places? (Chapters 24 and 26)........................

   ....

   (4) How does chapter 28 show that Saul had completely left God and turned to superstition?...
   What do you think of this witch? Was she a fake, or did God really allow her to bring Samuel up from the dead to talk to Saul?
   (5) How did Saul die?...

4. Note Saul's expressions of repentance. (24:16, 17; 26:17-25)
   Do you consider that he was truly repentant? Why?...

   ....

5. *Optional:* Try preparing this story as a radio script. Work the exciting and dramatic scenes into your story.

Does the title of this guide sheet agree with your own conclusions about Saul? Do you think Saul was to blame for the things that happened to him? Is a man a victim of circumstances or is he a victim of his own decisions?

THE BUILDER OF AN EMPIRE

The success of a nation depends to a great extent on its leaders. How do you account for David's success in building up this great nation? Upon what was he building?

I. A KING WITH HALF A KINGDOM (Read II Samuel 1—4)

1. Where was David crowned king? (2:1)
2. What tribe was loyal to him? (2:4)
3. Who was crowned king in the northern part of Israel?
4. What was the situation between the two kingdoms?
   Which was growing stronger?
5. Who was really the strength of the house of Saul?

6. What happened to cause the northern tribes to unite with David in one great kingdom?

7. What quality did David show in his treatment of his enemies?

II. THE BUILDING OF THE EMPIRE (II Samuel 5—10)

1. How long was David ruler in Hebron? In Jerusalem?
2. Why was it a good policy to move the capital to Jerusalem? Why was it a better location than Hebron?
3. David made Jerusalem a real capital by building a palace there (5:11, 12), and by moving the Ark of the Covenant into the city (6:2). Read chapter 6.
   What happened when a man put his hand on the ark? (6:6-11)

   In whose home was the Ark kept for a time?
   Notice the elaborate procession and celebration that accompanied the moving of the Ark into Jerusalem. (6:5, 14-19)
   Why was it so important to them to have the Ark in Jerusalem?

   Read Psalm 24. This was probably sung antiphonally as the procession climbed the hill to Jerusalem. Is it appropriate? Why?
4. Skim through chapter 8 to see how David conquered his enemies on all sides, and extended the boundaries of his empire so as to make it about five times the size of Saul's kingdom. List the nations that paid yearly tribute to David.

5. List the types of offices in David's political organization.

6. 8:15 is a good summary of the reign of David. What have you seen in his life that accounts for his success as a ruler?

DAVID'S SMALL KINGDOM AND HIS GREAT EMPIRE

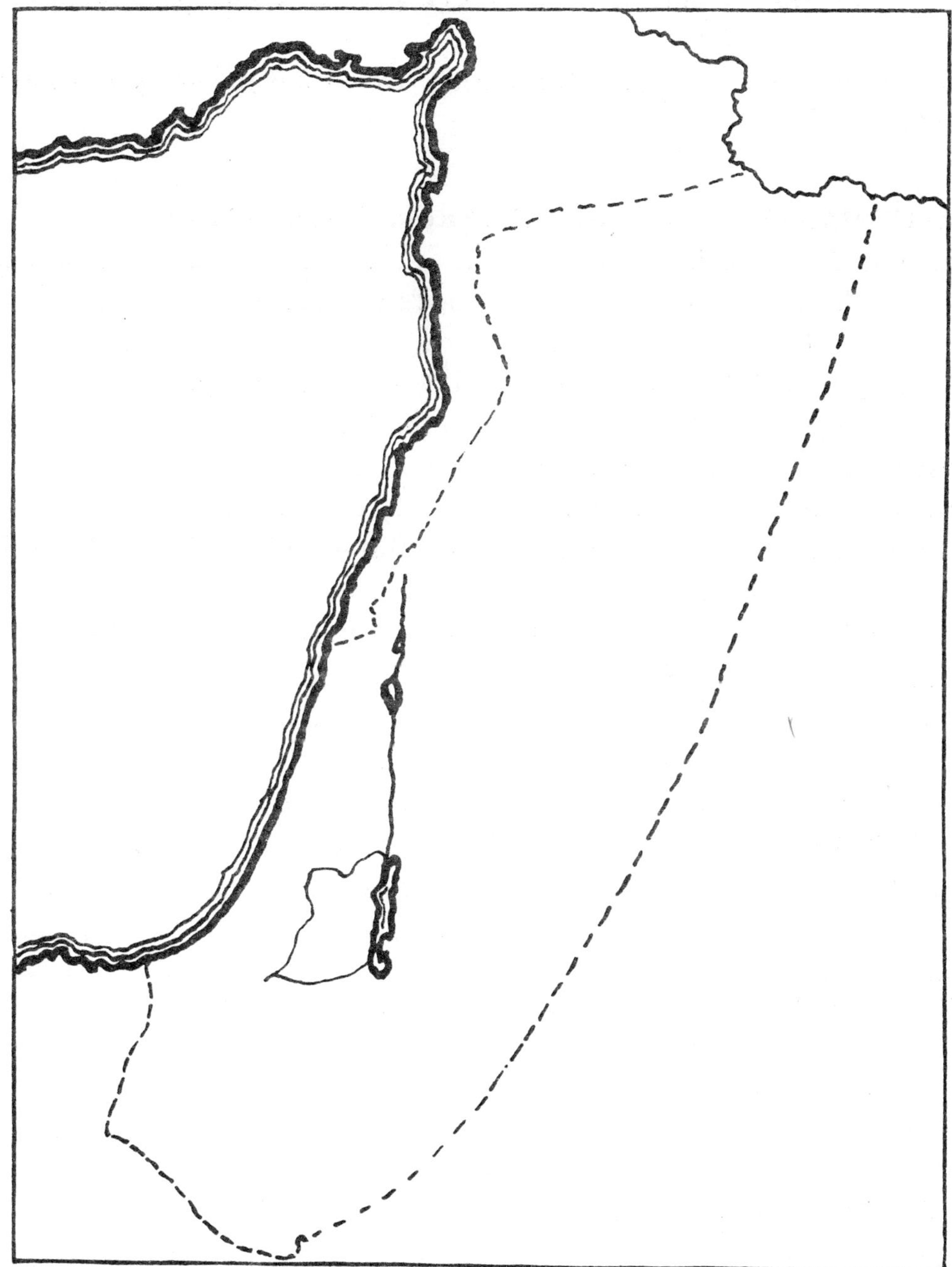

Label the small kingdom with which David began his rule, and the empire which he was able to build up. Color or shade the map to make the distinction clearer.

Consider the importance of David's relation to God in building this empire. List the principles or ideas this kingdom stood for in its time............

DAVID'S GREAT SIN AND ITS CONSEQUENCES

Does your wrongdoing matter to anyone but yourself? Does what you do have any effect on your family or your friends?

I. DAVID COMMITS A TERRIBLE SIN (Read II Samuel 11 and 12)

1. What was David's sin?
2. Who had the courage to tell the king of God's displeasure?
3. Why do you think he told David the story about the lamb?
4. What punishment did God send on David?
5. What punishment on his household?
6. What was David's attitude when accused of this sin? (Read Psalm 51, which may have been written on this occasion)

II. THE SIN AFFECTS DAVID'S HOUSEHOLD (Read II Samuel 13 and 14)

1. What sin did Ammon commit?
2. In what sense was David responsible?
3. What sin did Absalom commit?
4. In what way was family unity affected by this?

III. THE SIN BRINGS THE WHOLE NATION INTO CIVIL WAR

1. How did Absalom try to turn the people's hearts from his father? (15:1-6)
2. Where did Absalom go to be crowned king? (15:7-12)
3. How did David order his soldiers to treat Absalom? (18:5)
4. How was Absalom killed? (18:9-15)
5. David is one of the most grieved at the death of his faithless son. (18:33)
6. Note how the people returned to David after the war. (19:3)

IV. DAVID REPENTS OF HIS SIN

If David was truly repentant, how do you account for the drastic punishment that seems to have followed upon his sin? Does God forgive sin? Does God remove the consequences of sin? Read Psalms 51 and 32 in connection with this incident. What does each show about how David felt before and after his forgiveness by God?

1. Psalm 51
2. Psalm 32

SOLOMON'S TEMPLE

What is the purpose of a church building? How important was the Temple to Solomon and his people?

I. THE BUILDING OF THE TEMPLE
1. The contractor (I Kings 5:1, 2 and 7:13, 14) ....
2. The materials (5:6, 17 and 6:14-22) ....
   ....
3. The workmen (5:6, 15, 16) ....
4. Transportation of material (5:9) ....
5. The length of time needed (6:37, 38) ....
6. The dimensions of the Temple (A cubit is 18 inches) (6:2)
   .... x .... x ....
7. The furnishings of the Temple of ....(7:45) and of ....
   .... (7:48-50)

II. THE DEDICATION OF THE TEMPLE. Outline the program of the ceremony.
1. .... (8:1-4)
2. .... (8:5)
3. .... (8:10)
4. .... (8:14-21)
5. .... (8:22-53)
6. .... (8:55-61)
7. .... (8:65)

III. SOLOMON'S PRAYER OF DEDICATION
1. In spite of the magnificence of the Temple, Solomon realized that it could not be the actual dwelling place of God. What, then, was to be God's relationship to the house? (8:29, 30) ....
2. What reasons had Solomon for feeling that this House of God was worth while? What are some things he had found to be true of God? (8:23, 24, 56) ....
   ....
3. What was Solomon's purpose in building the Temple? (8:60) ....
   ....
4. List some of the circumstances under which people will want to come to this house to find God. (8:31, 33, 35, 37, 41-42, 44)
   ....
   ....

THE BOOK OF PROVERBS

The proverb is a short sentence conveying some moral truth or practical lesson in a concise, pointed form. What does the book of Proverbs teach on the following subjects? Put in your own words, or copy if brief enough.

1. Bad companions (1:10) ....

2. The value of an education (3:13-15) ....

3. Clean thinking and speaking (4:23, 24) ....

4. Laziness (6:6-8) ....

5. Religion in education (9:10) ....

Would Solomon have approved of taking Bible in high school? ....
6. Honesty (11:1) ....

7. Lying (12:22) ....

8. Courtesy (15:1) ....

9. Love (15:17) ....

10. Humility (16:18) ....

11. Self-control (16:32) ....

12. Drinking (20:1) ....

13. Reputation (22:1) ....

14. Treatment of enemies (25:21) ....

15. Minding your own business (26:17) ....

16. Contentment (30:8) ....

17. A picture of a worthy woman (31:10-31) ....

THE SPLENDOR OF THE GOLDEN AGE

To understand something of the splendor of Solomon and the Golden Age read quickly I Kings 1—11, concentrating on chapters 4 and 10. Try to get the following information:

1. What was the function of the twelve officers? (4:7, 27) ....

2. How big was Solomon's army? (10:26) ....

3. What was the purpose of his navy? (9:26-28; 10:22) ....

4. List some types of relationships he had with foreign nations.
   (1) .... (4:21)
   (2) .... (3:1; 9:16)
   (3) .... (10:1-10)
   (4) .... (11:1-3)

5. List some indications of peace and prosperity.
   (1) .... (4:24, 25)
   (2) .... (10:21)
   (3) .... (10:23-25)
   (4) .... (10:27)
   (5) .... (10:18-20)

6. List some things that show the wisdom of Solomon.
   (1) .... (3:5-28)
   (2) .... (4:29-34)
   (3) .... (10:3-7)

7. What were Solomon's methods of achieving this splendor?
   (1) From the foreign nations: (4:21) .... (9:20, 21) ....
   (2) Conscription of his own people (5:13-18): one month of every three in ....

8. How did Solomon secure provisions for his tremendous retinue? (4:7, 22, 23, 27) ....
   ....

9. Did the people feel burdened by the demands of the king? ....
   Read what they said to his son after Solomon's death (12:4) ....
   ....

10. Would you consider Solomon a dictator? .... Why? ....

If Samuel had been alive, could he not have said, "I told you so"? What is the real function of a leader in any group or nation?

The Divided Kingdom

THE DIVIDED KINGDOM: THE PRICE OF DICTATORSHIP

Upon what does the strength of a nation depend? What causes civil war? Why will not a dictatorship survive?

Read I Kings 11:26-43; chapters 12 and 14.

1. What was the purpose of the mass meeting at Shechem?...

2. Upon what condition were the people willing to accept Rehoboam as king?...

3. How can you explain the foolish advice of the young men?...

4. Try to discover why the people were ready to follow Jeroboam, a poor laborer, rather than Rehoboam, a prince. Summarize what you can find about the following:
   (1) His record as a workman (11:28)...
   (2) His fearlessness (11:26)..
   (3) His escape from the king (11:40)...
   (4) His concern for the people's welfare (12:1-4)..

5. If you had been an Israelite when your tribe was voting between Rehoboam and Jeroboam, which would you have chosen?..
   Why?...

6. Compare the two kingdoms in the following ways:

	JUDAH	ISRAEL
(1) The first king	Rehoboam	Jeroboam
(2) The number of tribes		
(3) The capital		
(4) Places of worship		
(5) Objects of worship		

   Note, however, that even Rehoboam allowed the worship of false gods.

7. What reason did Jeroboam give for setting up the worship of idols?..

Do you find anything that makes you think these two kingdoms will not last permanently? A comparison with the Golden Age of David may lead you to discover some of the disastrous weaknesses of the two kingdoms.

THE DIVIDED KINGDOM

1. Locate on the following map the empire of Solomon, the two kingdoms (Israel and Judah), the capital of each, and the places of worship in each.
2. Label the natural boundaries, the rivers, etc.

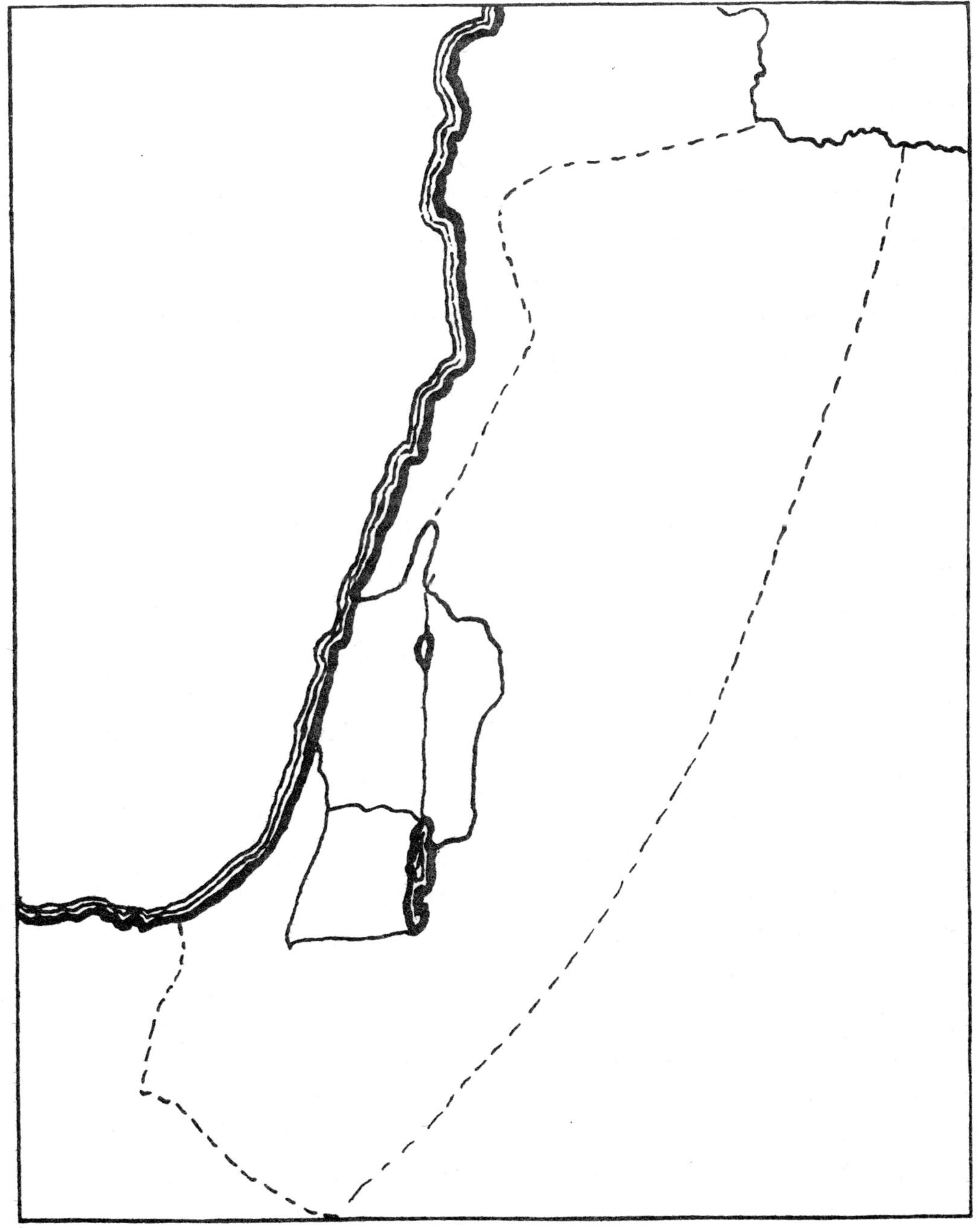

How did the idolatry of Solomon destroy the national unity and lead to the carelessness which made for the division of the kingdom? How does your worship affect your conduct?

THE TEST OF JEHOVAH

How do you account for the fearlessness of men who know that there is really a God?

Read I Kings 16—19

1. How did Omri, a military leader, secure the throne of Israel? (I Kings 16:16) ....
....

2. Note that he moved the capital from Shechem to .... (16:24)

3. What foreign policy of Solomon's for strengthening his kingdom was followed by Omri's son, Ahab? (16:31) ....

4. What effect did this have on the religion of Israel? List everything Jezebel did to substitute her religion of Baal for the worship of Jehovah.
   (1) .... (16:32)
   (2) .... (18:4)
   (3) .... (18:19)

5. What miracles had Elijah already worked to show that Jehovah was the only true God? See chapter 17.
   (1) ....
   (2) ....
   (3) ....

6. What indications can you find that Elijah's life was endangered by his standing up for his God? ....
....

7. Read chapter 18 for the story of the great contest between God and Baal.
   (1) What was Elijah's proposition to the people of Israel? (18:21, a.s.v.) "How long go ye limping between the two sides? if .... be God, ...: ....; but if ...., ..."
   (2) List details that show the distress of the priests at the silence of their god ....
....
   (3) List details that show the confidence of Elijah that his God could be counted on ....
....
   (4) What was the effect on the people? Quote their response to the miracle that followed.
....

How does God further reveal Himself to Elijah? (19:1-18) Note that He is more than a God of fire and earthquake and wind.

THE RETURN TO JEHOVAH-WORSHIP

How do you know there is a God? How can you persuade other people? What kind of God did Elijah think there was?

1. Read II Kings 1. How do you account for Elijah's severity in dealing with Ahaziah?..........

2. Read the story of the call of Elisha and the miraculous finish to Elijah's career as a prophet. (II Kings 2:1-18)

   What indications have you that God was real to these men?

3. List the miracles of Elisha recorded in II Kings 4 and 5.

4. Why was it important to the Israelites to have some visible signs of God's power at **this** particular time?

5. Read II Kings 9 and 10 for an account of Elisha's political activities.

   (1) What was his command to Jehu, the newly appointed king? (9:7-10)

   (2) How did Jehu justify his merciless killing of the royal families of Israel and Judah? (9:22)

   (3) By what trick did Jehu manage to kill all the remaining worshippers of Baal? (10:18-28)

*Think through this problem seriously. Was the "end" of religious reform important enough to use these violent means to bring it about? Try to think of reasons both for and against **this** action of Jehu. Have such methods been tried in other instances in history? With what success?*

A PROSPEROUS AND DECAYING NATION

What is the danger of prosperity? What may happen to a people who suddenly have more money than they are accustomed to? What else is necessary if a nation is going to survive?

1. During this period of her history Israel was frequently invaded by other nations, which were trying to enlarge their territory. Note indications of such an invasion in II Kings 13:1-7.
   (1) What nation? ....
   (2) Who was leader? ....
   (3) How much of an army was left to Israel? ....
   ....

2. Under the reign of Jeroboam II, however, there was a return to political power and material prosperity. List the signs of prosperity you find.
   (1) II Kings 14:25 ....
   (2) Amos 6:4-6 ....
   (3) Amos 3:15 ....

3. But the prosperity was accompanied by all sorts of evils. What are some of the evil practices you find in the following references?
   (1) Social injustice
       a. Amos 5:7 ....
       b. Amos 5:11 ....
       c. Amos 2:6 ....
   (2) Formal and empty religious ceremonies
       Amos 4:4, 5 ....
   (3) Careless leadership
       Hosea 4:1-14 ....

4. Think back to the Covenant promises of God and of the people. Are the people playing fair with God? ....

5. What has God warned them will have to be the consequences of this sort of life?
   ....

What will you as an individual learn from these experiences about the real values of life and the things you will live for?

AMOS'S CALL TO SOCIAL JUSTICE

Is a people's international power dependent on their national practices? Why? Does a nation's religion affect its relations to other countries?

1. Attempt to get a clear picture of Amos, the fiery prophet, who comes to these people to tell them about their wrongdoing.
   (1) His home town..(Amos 1:1) Look up on a map.
   (2) His occupation..(Amos 7:14)
   (3) God's call to him..(Amos 7:15)

2. Study the message of the prophet to the people at Bethel.
   (1) How does God feel about their oppression of the poor? (4:1-3)

   (2) How does God feel about their meaningless religious ceremonies?
   (5:21-24)..

   (3) What does he say is sure to happen to Israel? (5:27)

   (4) Pick out some expressions and comparisons which Amos used to persuade the people that destruction is an inevitable and necessary result of sin. (3:1-7)

   (5) What comparison does he use to show the completeness of their ruin? (3:12)................

   (6) How may the people prevent this catastrophe? (5:4-15)................

3. Study Amos's encounter with Amaziah, the priest.
   (1) What finally aroused the anger of the priest? (7:10, 11)

   (2) What command did he give Amos? (7: 12, 13)................

   (3) How do you account for the fearlessness of Amos?

4. Attempt to put in your own words the step Amos thought the Israelites should take to avoid the danger that threatened the nation.

5. Do you think his solution to the problem was a practical one?................
   Why?................

HOSEA'S PICTURE OF THE LOVE OF GOD

Does God love people even when they disobey Him? Will God always forgive? Will His love keep Him from punishing or make Him punish wrongdoing?

1. Read Hosea 1—3 to discover the tragedy that happened in Hosea's home.
   (1) What was the name of his wife?...................................
   (2) List the names of the three children and the meaning of each, if possible.

   a. ...., ...

   b. ...., ...

   c. ...., ...

   These names were given to suggest the unfaithfulness of the mother to her husband.
   (3) Gomer seems to have sunk to the low level of a slave as a result of her wretched life.
   How much did Hosea pay to rescue her from this condition?...
   (5) In what way is Israel like Gomer and God like Hosea?...
   (4) Do you respect Hosea for his great love for his wife?.................... Why?...................

   ....

   ....

   Note that Hosea narrated this family tragedy only to show Israel how she **herself had** been unfaithful to God.

2. Look up the following references to see what particular vices Israel had been **guilty of:**
   6:8.................................. 7:4.................................. 6:9..................................
   13:1, 2.................................. 4:1, 2.................................. 4:13..................................
   4:11..................................

3. What kind of punishment did Hosea see as an inevitable result of this kind of life? (11:5,6)
   ....

4. What is Hosea's continuous plea? (6:1; 14:1)
   ....

5. Read the following passages and list the characteristics of God which you think would mean most to the Israelites of Hosea's time: 11:1-4; 13:4-6; 14:4-9.

   ....

   ....

6. Memorize Hosea 6:6.

Do you think Hosea's proposed action was the way out of the national difficulty? Why?

THE FALL OF SAMARIA

But the people would not listen to the cry of the prophets.

Read II Kings 17.

1. In spite of the solution proposed by the prophets, Hoshea, the king of Israel, tried **another** way out of the national troubles. (17:3) What was the solution he tried?....................

2. But Hoshea could not be trusted. His treaty with Assyria was broken for a new treaty **with** another nation. What nation?....................

3. How did Assyria retaliate for Israel's broken treaty? (17:4-6)....................

4. Did God play fair with the Israelites in allowing this tragedy?
   Read 17:7-23 again to see what the author of II Kings thought.
   (1) What had Israel done that was wrong? (17:7-12) ....

   (2) Whom had God sent to show them the foolishness of their action? (17:13)....................

   (3) What had been the reaction of Israel to these men? (17:14-17)....................

   (4) What had God finally been forced to do? (17:18-23)....................

   Do you agree with the author of II Kings that God *had* to allow the captivity of His "Chosen People"? Under what conditions is punishment necessary?

5. What people were sent to settle in Samaria?....................
6. What kind of religion did these people have?....................
7. Do you see any "future" for the city of Samaria? ....
8. What have broken treaties to do with the religious faith of a nation?....................

In the long run, is what you do a clear indication of what you believe? Why?

THE RESCUE OF JERUSALEM BY A PROPHET

This is the story of the people of the Southern Kingdom, who were willing to listen to the prophet, at least for a time.

Read II Kings 18—20.

1. At the time of the fall of Samaria, capital of the Northern Kingdom, Hezekiah was the king of the Southern Kingdom.
   What sort of reforms do you find him carrying out in his kingdom? (18:1-6) ....

2. But what was his solution to the problem of Judah's relations with Assyria? (Read 16:7-9 for a note about the treaty his father Ahaz had made with Assyria.) How did Hezekiah handle this treaty? (18:7) ....

3. What was the action of the Assyrians in retaliation? ....

4. Who was the leader of the Assyrians at this time? ....

5. How much did Hezekiah's broken treaty cost him? (18:14-16) ....

6. What taunts did the Assyrians hurl at the God of the Israelites? (18:19-35; 19:10-13) ....

7. Note Hezekiah's complete trust in God. List the phrases in his prayer that impress you most in view of the mockery of the Assyrians. (19:15-19) ....

8. Who was the great prophet that brought to Hezekiah the assurance that God had heard his prayer and would answer it? ....

9. What happened to Sennacherib's army? ....

10. Compare the fall of Samaria with the rescue of Jerusalem. Do you find any evidence that the "way out" urged by Amos and Hosea was the real "way out"? ....

What is the secret of national strength today? Why do you think so?

ISAIAH, THE PROPHET OF A NEW DAY

Does God control everything that happens in the world? Does he ever take his hands off? Is it good news to the world or bad news that God is sovereign ruler of the world?

1. During this period in which the Assyrians have been attacking Israel, Isaiah the prophet was trying to keep Judah from falling prey to the same enemy.
   (1) Read Isaiah 31:1-3. What does Isaiah think of the policy of making a treaty with Egypt against the Assyrians?..

   (2) Read Isaiah 8:9-13. What other devices of Ahaz the king does Isaiah think will not be effective? ....

   (3) What is Judah's only hope of safety in this emergency?..

2. Read Isaiah 9:2-7 for the prophet's vision of a great day of peace when all men shall put their trust in God and He shall rule the nations. How will this future age differ from the age in which Isaiah is writing?..

3. Read Isaiah 11:1-9 for a second poem describing the King who is to come. These are usually considered "Messianic prophecies," or predictions of the coming of the Christ. What ideas do you find here which seem to you to be fulfilled in the life of Jesus?..

4. Isaiah's vision of the future was big enough to include the whole world. Read Isaiah 2:2-4.
   (1) What part will the worship of God play in the new world?..

   (2) What will be the rule of life by which the nations will live?..

   (3) Do you think Isaiah is right in thinking that this will bring peace?.................... Why or why not? ....

What assurance have we that some day God's rule will be effective throughout the world?

THE GREAT REFORM OF A BOY KING

What makes a king great? What sort of greatness did Napoleon have? Would Woodrow Wilson have made a good king? Why?

Read II Kings 22 and 23.

1. How old was Josiah when he became king of Judah?..

2. Glance through chapter 21 to see what kind of heritage he had received from his father and grandfather. Write down a few of the evils of their reigns..
    ....

3. How old was Josiah when he began to correct the bad conditions in his kingdom?................

4. Where did he begin his constructive work?...
    Can you think of any reason for this?...
    ....

5. What was found in the Temple when the building was being repaired?...................................
    What does this suggest about the condition of Temple worship previous to this time?............
    ....
    ....

6. What effect did the reading of this book have upon the young king?......................................
    Scholars think this was the book of Deuteronomy or part of it. Can you think of anything in the book that would distress the king? Glance back at Deuteronomy 29 and 30. Had Judah listened to these warnings?

7. What message did Huldah, the prophetess, send that confirmed the king's fear?...................
    ....

8. Did the king think of the national religion as his personal affair or as the affair of all the people? What did he do in 23:1-3 that shows his attitude?...
    Try to recall the various occasions on which the covenant has been renewed.

9. What practical things did the king do that showed that he took the covenant seriously? List several from 23:4-25 that seem important to you. ....
    ....

10. Do you think the praise of Josiah in 23:25 is more extravagant than he deserves?...............
    Why or why not?..
    ....

JEREMIAH'S PLEA FOR PERSONAL RELIGION

Can a nation know God if its individual citizens do not know Him?

1. Try to discover why Jeremiah felt that he *had* to become a prophet. (Jeremiah 1:1-10)
   (1) What was the occupation of the men of his family? (1:1) ....
   (2) Where did they live? ....
   (3) What kings were on the throne at the various times when the "word of the Lord" came to him? ....
   ....
   (4) How did he know that God had a special plan for his life? ....
   ....
   (5) What did he say that shows that he felt unworthy to be a prophet? ....
   ....

2. Josiah's reform did not last very long. What do you find in the following passages that shows that Judah had begun to worship idols again?
   (1) .... (7:18)
   (2) .... (7:31)

3. What was the effect of this idol worship on their lives?
   (1) .... (5:1)
   (2) .... (8:6)
   (3) .... (9:26)

4. What punishment was bound to come upon them according to Jeremiah?
   (1) .... (7:14, 15)
   (2) .... (27:6, 7)

5. But how does God feel about His people?
   (1) .... (31:1)
   (2) .... (31:20)

6. What kind of covenant did Jeremiah want the people to make with God? How does it differ from the earlier covenants they had made? (Jeremiah 31:31-34.)
   (1) Where will it be written? ....
   (2) How widespread will it be? ....
   (3) What will be the relationship of the people and God?
   I WILL BE .... AND THEY SHALL BE ....
   THEY SHALL ALL ....
   FOR I WILL ....

Do you agree with Jeremiah that the "way out" is a return to God?

THE DESTRUCTION OF JERUSALEM

But the people still would not listen!

Read II Kings 25 as many times as necessary to get a clear picture of the fall of the great city of Jerusalem. List the major events.

Select one of the following projects as a record of what happened:

1. Prepare a newspaper account of the capture of Jerusalem such as might have appeared in the *Jerusalem Times*. Some such headlines as the following might suggest the sort of article you will want to write. Let your imagination work!

KING NEBUCHADNEZZAR APPROACHES JERUSALEM

FAMINE CONTINUES UNCHECKED. SIEGE UNBROKEN

ESCAPE OF MILITARY LEADERS FROM JERUSALEM

KING ZEDEKIAH TAKEN PRISONER. SONS SLAIN

VINDICTIVE BABYLONIANS BLIND KING ZEDEKIAH

NEBUCHADNEZZAR MERCILESS IN TREATMENT OF KING

FIRE RAGES THROUGH JERUSALEM

TEMPLE AND PALACE RAZED TO GROUND

POPULATION OF CITY DEPORTED TO BABYLON

2. Write an editorial such as might have been written by one of the priestly class during the siege of Jerusalem. This might include a criticism of the king's foreign policy, a summary of the message of the prophets, a reminder of the fall of Samaria about 150 years before.

3. Write an article such as might have been written by Gedaliah (vs. 22) to encourage the people who were left in the land of Judah.

4. Write a letter that might have been written by one of the boys or girls left in the land of Judah to a cousin who was deported to Babylon.

The Captivity of the Hebrew People

THE LIFE OF A CAPTIVE IN BABYLON

How would you feel if you were a prisoner of war? How did these people feel? What did they miss most? What would you?

1. The Bible does not contain a simple, clear story of what happened in Babylonia. You will have to look for facts about life in Babylon in some Bible history or other reference book. Try to get the following information:

    (1) The location of the Jewish colony...

    (2) What Babylon was like...

    ....

    (3) The changes that took place in Israel's economic life in Babylon...............

    ....

    (4) The changes in their religious ideas......... ....

    ....

    (5) What the synagogue was...

    (6) The kind of religious writing done during this period...........................

    ....

2. But the Bible does tell us clearly how they felt about this exile. Discover as much as you can about the feelings of these deported people. Read the suggested Psalms and summarize in your own words how the people felt.

    (1) Their homesickness for Jerusalem (Psalm 137) ....

    ....

    (2) Their realization that they deserved what they got (Psalm 130).................

    ....

    ....

    (3) Their confidence that God will rescue them (Psalm 130).........................

    ....

    ....

3. Is it possible that this catastrophe of the destruction of Jerusalem will be a good thing for the Hebrew nation after all? Why? Might it lead to a "new covenant" such as is pictured in Jeremiah 30, 31? Discuss the possibilities as you see them...............................

    ....

    ....

THE CAPTIVITY

1. On the maps below label the rivers and other bodies of water.
2. Locate the place where the Hebrews lived while in captivity.
3. Indicate by shading or coloring the extent of the Babylonian and Persian Empires.

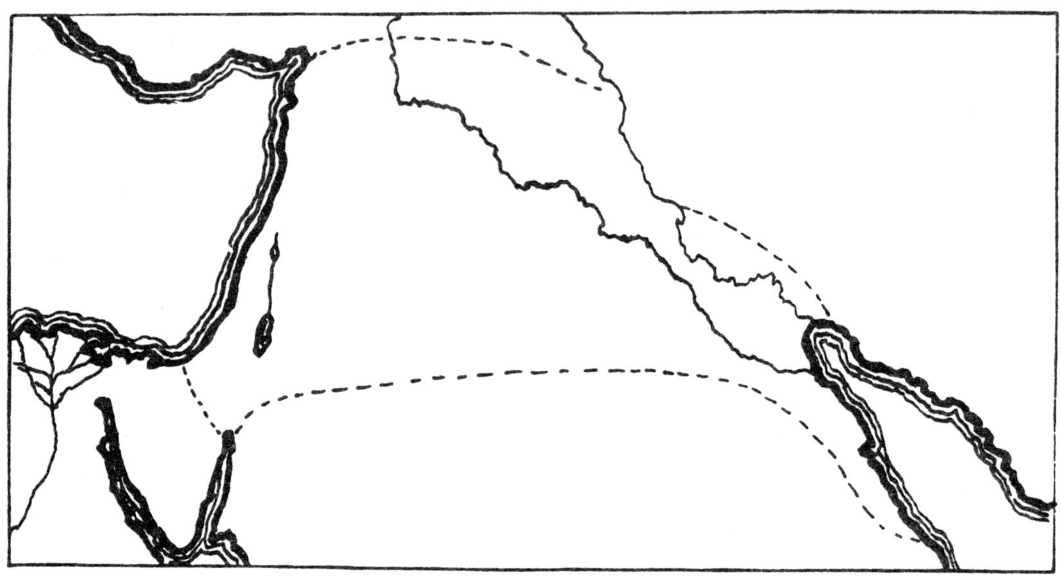

MAP VII   *The Babylonian Empire*

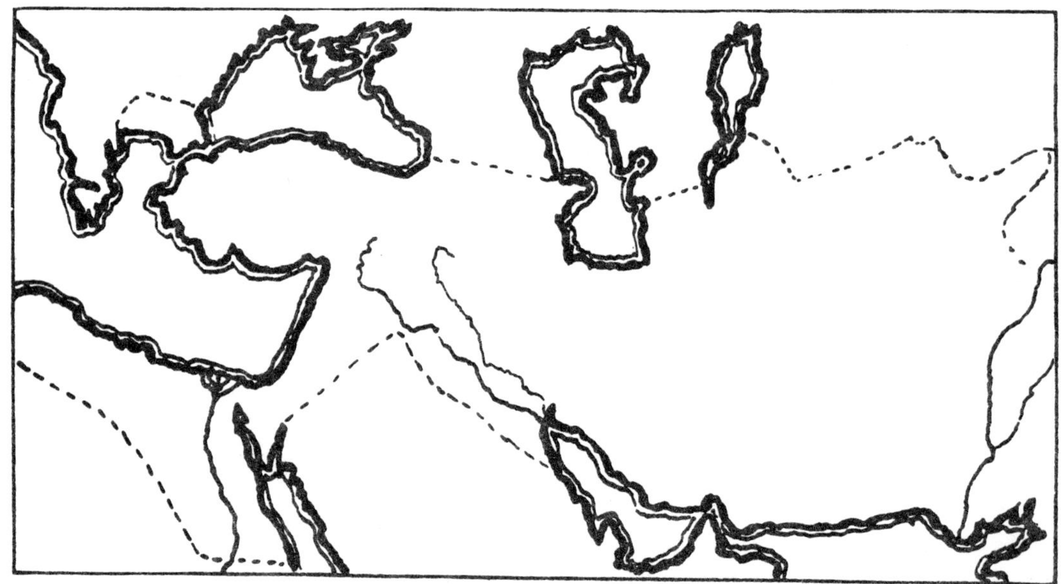

MAP VIII   *The Persian Empire*

Why were the Hebrew people taken into captivity? What good end might come out of this tragedy?

EZEKIEL, THE WATCHMAN OF GOD

Never before had the Israelites wanted so desperately to be sure that there was a God who would hear them.

1. Look for the way God's call came to Ezekiel. Read Ezekiel 1:1—3:15.
   (1) Where was Ezekiel located? (1:1) ....
   (2) How long had the Israelites been in captivity? (1:2) ....
   (3) How much are we told about the appearance of Jehovah in this vision? (1:26-28)
   ....
   (4) To whom was Ezekiel instructed to speak? (2:3-7; 3:4-11) ....
   ....
   (5) Will Ezekiel be a popular preacher? ....
   (6) What did God mean in calling him a "watchman"? (3:16-21) ....
   ....

2. Study Ezekiel 18:1-32. Look for a new religious idea that Ezekiel taught the Israelites.
   (1) What proverb had been often quoted in Israel? (18:2) ....
   ....
   (2) Had it proved true in the destruction of Jerusalem? Had the innocent suffered with the guilty? Had children paid for their fathers' sins? ....
   (3) What new principle does Ezekiel preach now? ....
   ....

   Do you consider this an important thing for men to know about God's way of dealing with people? Why? In what way does it make an individual feel more responsible for what happens to him?

3. In what pictorial way did Ezekiel give hope to the Israelites that they would be rescued from this captivity in Babylonia? Read Ezekiel 37.
   (1) Who are the "dry bones"? ....
   (2) List several definite things that Ezekiel promised the people that God would do for them. (37:21-23) ....
   ....
   (3) How does God feel about His people? (34:11-16) ....
   ....
   (4) What change will God bring about in His people? (36:25-27) ....
   ....

Have you ever looked back on some calamity in your life and felt that it was a good thing after all?

A PROPHET OF COMFORT

Can you think of examples of one person suffering for the sake of another? Is there any greater illustration of love, do you think?

1. Read Isaiah 40:1-11. List the phrases that you think would mean most to the captive Israelites.

2. What kind of God does this prophet tell about? How does He compare with other gods? List the phrases that describe what God really is like. (40:12-31)

3. The prophet tells the people that God will use Cyrus of Persia to accomplish His purpose for this people. What will Cyrus do? (45:1-4; 45:11-13)

4. What will be Israel's role in the new world God will establish? (41:8-10)

5. How widespread is their work to be? Among what people? (49:1-6)

6. What will they tell the world about God? (44:1-8)

Does this book of "II Isaiah" help you to understand the purpose of God in having a "chosen nation"? Does God love all people equally? If so, what explanation can you give for His having "chosen" one special nation for His care?

7. But the prophet sees that such a great service to mankind can be accomplished only at a great sacrifice. What do we mean by "vicarious suffering"? Look up in a dictionary.

8. Read Isaiah 52:13—53:12 aloud several times. Some scholars think the "Suffering Servant" refers to Israel, the suffering nation; others think it is a definite prophecy of the suffering and redeeming Messiah that is to come.

    (1) What kind of suffering do you find here?

    (2) For whom was it endured?

    (3) What was the sufferer's attitude toward suffering?

    (4) What was accomplished by the suffering?

    (5) List the phrases in this prophecy that suggest to you events in the life and death of Jesus as you know them.

THE CAPTIVITY OF ISRAEL AND JUDAH

(A Summary of Events)

The Captivity of Israel

Samaria was destroyed and the people of Israel were carried away to Assyria in 722 B. C. These 10 tribes were scattered and are still known today as the lost Ten Tribes of Israel.

The Captivity of Judah

The people of Judah were carried captive to Babylon in three groups:

1. 605 B. C. Daniel and others were carried from Jerusalem to Babylon.
2. 597 B. C. The king of Judah and many of his people were carried to Babylon.
3. 586 B. C. Jerusalem was destroyed, the Temple burned, and most of the people were carried to Babylon.

These two tribes were allowed to settle in groups among the Babylonians and kept their identity as a Jewish people.

Benefits of the Captivity

1. Idolatry was destroyed. Never again did the Hebrew nation worship any god but Jehovah.
2. Public worship was established. The people, being away from the Temple of their own, began to assemble for reading the Law of Moses and for prayer. These gatherings are believed to have been the beginning of the Jewish Synagogue.
3. There was a new longing for the Messiah.

Return from Captivity.

The Jews returned to Jerusalem in three expeditions:

1. In 538 B. C. Cyrus of Persia, now ruler of Babylon, issued a decree permitting the Jews to return to Jerusalem. About 43,000 people returned under the leadership of Jerubbabel.
2. In 458 B. C. during the reign of Artaxerxes of Persia 60,000 people returned under the leadership of Ezra.
3. In 445 B. C. during the reign of Artaxerxes a group returned under Nehemiah for the purpose of rebuilding the walls of Jerusalem and re-establishing the nation.

Judah and some from other tribes returned to Palestine. The people were called "Jews" from this time on.

UNIT XI

The Restoration of Jerusalem

THE RETURN TO JERUSALEM

Can you think of any migrations of people for the sake of religion? Compare the Israelites with the Pilgrims.

Read Ezra 1.

1. What new king had come to power over the captives in Babylon? (Ezra 1:1) ....Look back at Map VIII for the extent of the great Persian Empire.
2. What was the policy of this king toward the foreign people living in his empire? Summarize the proclamation he made to the Israelites.

3. How did the king help the trip financially?..

4. How many people are reported to have returned to Jerusalem? (Ezra 2:64) ....
5. Who were the leaders of the pilgrimage? (Ezra 3:1, 2)...

6. Read chapter 3. How do you explain the fact that the first thing they did on arrival was to worship God?...

7. What was the feeling of the people on seeing the foundations of the Temple?.................

   Read Psalms 84, 85, 87, to see how the people felt.
8. Read chapters 4—6 rapidly. How do you account for the trouble they had in rebuilding the Temple?...

9. What prophets do you find as leaders of the people? (Ezra 5:1)

10. What message of comfort did Haggai bring when the building program was delayed? (Read Haggai 1:1—2:9, especially 1:13 and 2:4)
11. What promise did Zechariah make about the future of Jerusalem? (Zechariah 1:14, 16, 17)..
12. What kind of greatness did he want for this famous city?
    (1)...(8:3)
    (2)..(8:4, 5)
    (3)...(8:12)
    (4)...(8:16)
    (5)...(8:20-22)

THE REBUILDING OF JERUSALEM

What different kinds of building will be necessary in a postwar world? Is a city rebuilt when its walls and buildings are restored?

1. What made Nehemiah decide to leave Persia and go to Jerusalem? (Nehemiah 1) ....
....

2. *Optional:* Read Malachi's record of the conditions in Jerusalem to see whether the report that came to Nehemiah was true. (Malachi 1—3)
....

3. How did King Artaxerxes receive Nehemiah's request for permission to go? (Nehemiah 2:1-11) ....

4. How did Nehemiah go about his work of rebuilding? List the steps he took.
   (1) Nehemiah 2:12-16..
   (2) Nehemiah 2:17-20..
   (3) Do you consider Nehemiah a wise administrator?.................... Why?....................
   ....

5. How did Nehemiah explain the remarkable success of the people in building the wall? (Nehemiah 4:6)
   ....

6. How did they meet the opposition of the neighboring people? (4:15-21)....................
   ....
   ....

7. How did Nehemiah keep the wealthy people from taking advantage of the poor? (5:1-13)
   ....
   ....
   What do you think of Nehemiah's "New Deal"? ....

8. What example did he himself set? (5:14-18)..
   ....

9. What regulations did he make to keep the people from violating the Sabbath day? (13: 15-21)
   ....

10. What was his attitude toward marriages with foreign women? (13:23-30)....................
    ....

What do you think of the reforms that Nehemiah tried to carry out? Do you think he was on the right track? Had the history of Israel up to this time given him any reason for thinking these things important?

THE STORY OF ESTHER

Read the book of Esther straight through. See what you can do with the story by thinking of it as a play.

1. Describe briefly each of the following characters as if for a "play bill" or program. Add any other characters you think necessary.

Dramatis Personnae

Ahasuerus ....

Vashti ....

Mordecai ....

Esther ....

Haman ....

Chamberlains, scribes, servants

2. Write a synopsis of the play, summarizing the action of each scene as suggested by the titles below:

SCENE I.   The King's Beauty Contest (Chapters 1-2)

SCENE II.   Esther's Decision (Chapters 3-4)

SCENE III.   Haman's Disappointment (Chapters 5-6)

SCENE IV.   Esther's Banquet (Chapters 7-8)

THE PERIOD BETWEEN THE TESTAMENTS

The Old Testament closes about a hundred years after the Jews' return from the captivity under Cyrus of Persia. The "four hundred silent years" are the next 400 years before the New Testament opens with its stories of the birth of Christ. It was silent only in that the events of the period are not recorded in the Bible. Actually many momentous historical events took place, and Palestine was the center or the battleground for this period. It is a miracle that the remnant of Israel survived at all.

Perhaps a summary of the period may help you to see it more clearly:

The Assyrian Empire	900 - 605 B. C.
The Babylonian Empire	605 - 539 B. C.
The Persian Empire	539 - 331 B. C.
The Greek Empire	331 - 166 B. C.
The Maccabean Period	166 - 37 B. C.
The Roman Empire	37 B. C.

(The above dates are from *The Westminster Dictionary of the Bible,* by John D. Davis, revised and rewritten by Henry Snyder Gehman.)

The Northern Kingdom had been captured and carried away into Exile during the Assyrian Period, the Southern Kingdom during the Babylonian Period. Then Cyrus of Persia had overcome the Babylonians and set up his Persian Empire. His policy toward captive people had been more liberal than that of the two preceding empires, and he allowed the Jews to return to their own land and there set up their nation and re-establish their religion, all as a part of his great empire. During this period the Jews were allowed a great amount of freedom.

In 331 Alexander the Great overthrew the Persian rule and came into possession of Palestine. At his death the Greek Empire was divided among his four generals, Syria going to Seleucus and Egypt to Ptolemy. Palestine, being between the two, was claimed by both. It was ruled by the Ptolemies 323-198 B. C., and by the Seleucids 198-164 B. C. Antiochus Ephphanes, one of the Seleucids, attempted to spread Greek culture and religion in Palestine. He forbade the worship of Jehovah and placed a statue of Jupiter in the altar in the Temple. Heathen altars were set up in every town, and anyone discovered in possession of the Old Testament was put to death.

This led to the Maccabean Revolt. Mattathias, a priest, rebelled against this persecution and managed to raise an army with the help of his sons, who were called Maccabees, or the "Hammerers," because of the way they fought. They drove out the Syrian army and established an independent Jewish nation for about one hundred years. The priests ruled during this period with political as well as religious power, and the hopes of a Messiah rose again. But trouble arose between two brothers among the priests, and they appealed to the Romans to settle the difficulty.

The Romans settled it by capturing Jerusalem in 63 B. C. and making all of Palestine a part of the Roman Empire. In 37 B. C. Herod the Great was appointed king of the Jews and he was on the throne when the New Testament opens with the birth of Jesus.

SUGGESTIONS FOR INDIVIDUAL PROJECTS

Each student may select one project for individual work during the semester. The following are merely suggestive. Do not feel that you must be limited to these items.

1. A collection of pictures or drawings illustrating the stories.
2. Armchair travels through Bible lands. Maps with descriptions or stories of the places shown.
3. Who's Who in the Bible.
4. Collection of poems, hymns, and literary references in English and American literature arranged in order of the Bible story.
5. Model of the Tabernacle. (Group project)
6. Manners and customs of the Hebrews illustrated and explained, tools, musical instruments, weapons, homes, clothes, etc.
7. Believe It or Not. (Illustrated, if possible)
8. The Hebrew Hall of Fame. The great men and women of the Old Testament with a sketch of each, showing why chosen.
9. A chart or diagram of each book of the Bible studied.
10. Memory work. 100 Bible verses chosen from approved passages. Hymns.
11. Scenario or Dramatization. One long play showing a whole book. Three or more shorter ones.
12. A play written, costumed, and produced. (Group project)
13. A series of illustrated maps. (See Egermeier's *Bible Story Book*)
14. A collection of Bible games or riddles.
15. Outside reading. Three approved books read and reported on.
16. A series of 10 or more character sketches like the following:
    Abraham, a Man of Vision.
    Joseph—How a Spoiled Boy Became a Leader
    Saul, the Self-Made Fool
    The Call of Moses. Does God have a plan for every life?
17. A series of 10 or more editorials that might have appeared in a newspaper in Egypt, Moab, or Canaan, such as:
    In praise of Joseph, the new food administrator.
    Shall the Hebrews have a monarchy?
    Against conscription.
18. A series of 10 or more news articles like the above.
19. A series of 10 or more discussions showing the development of the Hebrews, such as:
    What the Hebrews learned about God in Genesis.
    The advantages to the Hebrews of living in Egypt.
    Some archaeological findings.